INSIGHT

Business Advice in an Age of Complexity

BY DAVID WIMER
WITH ROBERT F. EVERETT PH.D.

First Edition

Published by David Wimer Advisors, LLC, Sinking Spring, PA
T: 484-269-7700 F: 610-678-5068 E: insight@davidwimer.com

Manufactured & Produced in the United States of America

ISBN-10: 0615906516
ISBN-13: 9780615906515
Library of Congress Control Number: 2013919142
David Wimer Advisors, LLC, Sinking Spring, PA

Per Angusta ad Augusta

[Through Trials To Triumph]

Dedication

This book has been percolating over 35 years of business ownership. I am deeply grateful for those who have helped me on my path of business owner, professional manager and advisor. I dedicate this book to all those who have made my work possible:

To my clients and owners with whom I worked closely, I thank you for your confidence in me to tackle some intensely difficult challenges on your behalf. Your belief in our potential has led us to some remarkable accomplishments together.

To all the employees I've been fortunate to associate with and lead in business, I appreciate that you chose to be on our journey, in good times and in challenging times. I admire your trust and investment of heart, hands and minds to overcome significant odds. Always believe in small miracles.

To my former business partners, I am grateful for the time we shared together and for your contributions to my body of knowledge and advisory experiences. Thank you for providing me the opportunity to grow professionally. It was invaluable.

To my editors: Jeff Klunk, Jim Bennett, Gary Rogers, Kevin Hollinger, Jenna Lombardo, and Larry Fegley. I am deeply appreciative of your careful and thoughtful efforts in helping me shape this book into what it is today.

To my co-author Bob Everett with whom I have enjoyed a collegial relationship for the past eight years. Your commitment to organize my body of work, provide it structure and find my voice has been very meaningful to me. Not only has our work been personally joyful, it has been a worthy endeavor.

To my Four Mentors: Dad, Gene, Jeff, and Fred (in memoriam), who have had a significant influence in my personal and business life. Because of your inspiration, I hope to pass along what I learned to another generation of business owner.

Mom and Dad, I have always known that someday I would write. I've been luckier than most in a choice we never get -- our parents. Your artfulness and financial acumen respectively have blessed me with a rare mix of creative financial insight. I hope you see your gifts revealed in my life's work.

To my children Jennifer, Nicki, Emily & Eric, I am deeply proud of who you are as individuals, and hope that I have provided guidance and a spirited path to make a difference in your lives. May each of you find the same bliss in your chosen vocation that I have in mine.

And finally to my wife Toni, who accepts me for my entrepreneurial spirit as a dreamer and a doer. My career and our journey together would best be described as an adventure and it has only been possible because I could count on you as my anchor in life and best friend.

I'm a very lucky guy who works hard at being the best he can be, serving others as a Business Advisor. I wouldn't have scripted my life any other way.

David Wimer

Table of Contents

DEDICATION V

CHAPTER 1: INTRODUCTION 1
    Why I Wrote This Book 1
    Business as a Way of Life 2
    Complexity as a Way of Life 3
    Navigating Transition 5
    Challenges I have Faced as an Advisor 7
    The Paradox of Comfort... 9
    The Practice of Business Advice.. 10
    The Financial Value of Advice 13
    Overview of This Book 15

CHAPTER 2: THE BLESSINGS OF AN ORDINARY LIFE 19
    An Ordinary Life 19
    The Four Mentors 21
        Fred: The Outdoorsman.. 22
        Dad: The Financial Chief 23
        Gene: The Entrepreneur... 24
        Jeff: The Merlin.. 26
    The Path of Entrepreneur 29
    Eating Humble Pie 30
    The Path of Professional Manager 33
    The Epiphany of Primary Care 36
    The Path of Advisor... 38

CHAPTER 3: WHY OWNERS SEEK ADVICE 41
    Introduction.. 41
    Transition Points for Advice 42

Benefits of Advice 46

Informal Networks 48

Formal Networks 50

CHAPTER 4: THE SCIENCE OF BUSINESS ADVICE 53

The Science of the Brain 53

It May Be All In the Mind 53

Get a Myelin Wrap 54

The Meddling Conscious 55

The Team of Rivals 56

Mastering Practice 59

Personal Creativity 61

CHAPTER 5: THE ROLES OF AN ADVISOR 63

The Inspired Generalist 63

The Roles of an Advisor 64

The Advisor Role 64

The Consultant Role 65

The Coach Role 65

Professional Advice 67

Internal & External Advisors 70

Internal Advisors 71

Strengths of an Internal Advisor 72

Weaknesses of an Internal Advisor 72

External Advisors 73

Strengths of an External Advisor 74

Weaknesses of an External Advisor 75

The Case for Engagement 76

Opening the Door to Possibilities 77

Advisor as Generalist 78

Advice in Business 79

CHAPTER 6: WHEN BUSINESS ADVICE MATTERS MOST 81

The Business Ownership Lifecycle 81

Starting a Business 81

Staying in Business.. 82

Transitioning a Business... 82

Planning the Exit 83

Selling the Company 85

Keeping the Company.. 86

Dissolving the Company.. 86

Value Creation 87

Crisis Response 88

Getting Unstuck 88

Planning for Contingencies 89

Lost Opportunities 90

Negative Events 90

Setting a Vision 91

Diversifying the Company... 92

Acquiring a Company 93

Setting Goals... 94

The Five Step Goal Setting Process 95

Goal Conflicts... 102

Impacting the Ownership Lifecycle........................... 105

Planning for Change 105

Preparing for Transition.. 107

CHAPTER 7: BUSINESS ADVICE KILLERS.......................... 109

Introduction 109

Why Owners Resist Advice 109

Ego... 110

Bad Experience 111

Ready, Fire, Aim 112

I Can't Afford It 112

Maintaining Control and Insecurity 114

Emotional Pitfalls 115

Looking for Results in All the Wrong Places 117

The Trouble with Numbers 119

Be Careful What You Measure 122

The Impact of Fear 122

Fear and the Downward Spiral 124

The Impact of Inertia 129

The Impact of Other Blockages 132

CHAPTER 8: MAKING ADVICE WORK 135

Introduction 135

Leading Change 136

Leading With Heart 138

People First, Always 140

Relying On Others 141

Relying On Strengths 144

Achieving Engagement 146

Building Momentum 148

Measuring Progress 150

Engaging Stakeholders 152

Making Advice Work 153

CHAPTER 9: THE GUIDING VIRTUES OF ADVICE 155

Fred: The Outdoorsman 156

Dad: The Financial Chief 156

Gene: The Entrepreneur 157

Jeff: The Merlin 157

Adaptability 158

Compassion 161

Curiosity 164
Accountability 167
Humility 170
Integrity 174
Connectedness 176
Passion 178
Resourcefulness..180
Acceptance 183
Contemplation 188
Intuition 190
Patience 192

CHAPTER 10: ON BECOMING AN ADVISOR - A PRIMER 195
Introduction 195
Becoming an Advisor 196
The Role of the Advisor...197
The Advisory Engagement 200
  The Beginning...*200*
  The Project...*202*
  Expectations & Metrics.....................................*207*
  The End of a Project...*208*

CHAPTER 11: REFLECTIONS ON INSIGHT & ADVICE 211
Leading Business Change 211
Business Transformation..213
Building on Trust 215
Pulling Together 216
The Challenges Forward 218
Coda...221

Chapter 1: Introduction

❖ ❖ ❖

Why I Wrote This Book

This book was written about the business and personal experiences I have had over 35+ years as a business owner, professional manager and advisor, using insight as a tool to sort through business complexity.

There are several reasons why I wrote this book at this time in my life. Part of me just wanted to share my journey with my family and friends. Part of me thought that my insights might be valuable to others in business, especially business owners and the professionals who work with them. Also, I just wanted to prove to myself I could do it. Whatever the reason, I knew that I would feel somehow diminished if this critical item on my "bucket list" were not completed.

I am grateful that my wife Toni encouraged me to put myself out there, and not to assume that what I have learned is commonplace. My co-author Bob Everett supported pursuit of my most personal experiences because he felt it would make a difference if readers understood how I had come to be where I am and who I am. Bob has been patient with me as I opened my shells of captured experience to find seeds of unconventional business practice, insight, and wisdom.

In this book I share stories of emotionally-charged business situations where owners thought were destined for disaster but, instead, experienced a new business life. And I will share how these transitions and circumstances were confronted, transcended, and transformed, often under immensely difficult and emotionally-intense conditions.

Whether or not you are facing an uncomfortable business circumstance or an exciting business transition at this moment is irrelevant. When you do (because you eventually will) you may wish to use some of the insights in my own business journey as a reference point, a stake in the ground.

Business as a Way of Life

I earn my living as a Business Advisor, helping (mostly family) businesses with issues of survival, growth, and/or transition. I work on business matters that affect financial performance and business value.

**I am engaged for my ability to provide unforeseen
options using my insights into finance, people,
and broad-based business operations.**

I care about my clients and they feel comfortable with me. They rely on me. I am also their best advocate. I am at times a friend, an accountant, a contract administrator, a parent, a negotiator, an agent, a confessor, a marriage counselor, and a warrior. I do whatever it takes. And, in doing so, I have learned a great deal about the practice of being in business as a way of life.

This book is also about how I came to be a Business Advisor. Early on in my career I looked at a couple career roads to travel and picked one, notably for the wrong reasons. It somehow turned out right. It's one of the many paradoxes of my life. I happened to land in business.

2

Complexity as a Way of Life

I can look back at my early years of starting in business where it seemed like owning and operating a business was a simple way of life. It was enjoying the craft of business and managing the known risks. I could count on myself and my know-how to carry me through almost any difficulty. I had a willingness to work harder than competitors, for longer hours, and that would generally provide the profit to care for my family. There was also the anticipation of the eventual big payday when the business would be sold. With the help of a business lawyer and an accountant for occasional advice, I paid attention to my craftsmanship, fueled by my passion for the work and the rest generally took care of itself. Business moved at a predictable pace and so did life in general. But that's when business life was simple.

Thirty-five years later we now live in an age of increased and increasing business complexity. That complexity is driven by ongoing technology leaps and vast increases in the volume of information accessible at our finger tips. However, the speed that business is conducted today is a double-edged sword. We are more technologically connected but have become personally disconnected. Who would have considered in the 1980's the business and social impacts of the Internet or texting?

Other dynamic changes have also occurred. We see shortened product and service lives and transformational shifts in markets occur in compressed timeframes. Look at how mortgage backed securities and the housing value bubble affected our home values. We can be influenced regionally by a global economy. Consider the impacts of metals manufacturing in China and the decline of precision machining domestically in the last ten years. Business owners are pressed to remain vigilant at all times for competitors who are smarter, more agile, and hungry to grow their market share. Higher stakeholder expectations and profit demands are also being placed on business financial performance. Overall these and many more external pressures add to business complexity. I will address these in more detail later in the book.

Equally as important to external influences they face, business owners are being impacted by what is going on inside their organization:

- Healthcare mandates
- Compliance issues
- Legal liabilities
- Cyber liability insurances
- Government intervention
- Productivity demands
- Operational efficiency requirements
- Supply chain compression
- Profit margin reductions
- Personnel development

It is this age of driving business faster and better that creates this complexity. Few, if any, of us have been trained to deal with it.

Personally we are living longer as a result of better pharmacology, advances in medical technology and disease testing, and awareness of exercise and nutrition. We are becoming increasingly aware of the effects of mental health in society. The media has brought us the instant randomness of terror initiated by a religious group, a tornado, or a deranged individual. And we are debating heatedly on what to do about it. We see social complexities arise with on-line lists of sexual predators living in our neighborhood, or news of a bully at school that delivers mobile texts that result in suicide. Alcohol and drug abuse contribute to avoidance of issues in our business and personal lives, as well as creating huge sets of problems of their own. There's no doubt that as business owners we feel the personal impacts of these unsettling social changes.

It is how we, as leaders, respond and adapt to these business and personal complexities that is the essential challenge at hand.

And that is why I want to share my perspective on insight as a guide to navigating the change that confronts the business owner.

Navigating Transition

I call these points of change in business "transitions." Business transitions have the potential to significantly impact business owners, their families, their ongoing livelihoods, and the overall value of their businesses. Securing an economic future by owning a business means living with and adapting to the demands and risks of business transitions.

Transitions in business and life come in two flavors – those we select and those we don't select.

And in both circumstances, more than ever before, we need objective insight to guide our decisions. Insight can help provide answers to how we might adjust and adapt to changing circumstances. Success requires the ability to look beyond one's personal experience, education, preconceptions, and beliefs, to see and appreciate what is actually going on. The question becomes, is what we are seeing real or is it a creation of our own limiting beliefs and perspectives? By rigorously acknowledging the business transition circumstances, an owner may see her way to a solution more clearly.

It's not what happens to us that makes the difference, but rather it's how we respond, adapt, adjust and transcend these transition points.

Sometimes transition points are not so obvious. Sometimes a critical transition point may be experienced as a lingering malaise or inability to jump start financial performance. It may be difficult for an owner to pinpoint the specific problem area or opportunity because of the noise of day-to-day operations. It is at these times that objective insight is most helpful to an owner. An objective, third party view helps to assess and describe the underlying challenges and to pose alternative options and possibilities that remain hidden to the owner.

The task of confronting an owner's new reality is also filled with emotion. When contemplating seeking objective advice, owners often tell themselves:

- "It's my baby."
- "I'm too close to it."
- "I'm concerned about letting go."
- "I'm not sure they will be able to do it like I do it."
- "If I can't fix it no one can."

For instance, there are times the owner must cross a chasm of uncertainty, such as in the sale of a business. There are times when important succession decisions require in-depth, confidential discussions (e.g., financial payouts) that may have long-term consequences to the owner. And there are times (e.g., an acquisition) where things may appear to be going along quite smoothly yet underneath it all, there is unrest and employee resistance.

Significant, anxiety-provoking events are tricky to deal with alone.

There's another option for business owners that would like to have assistance in navigating these transitions or circumstances that are thrust upon them. And that option is the insight of a Business Advisor.

Challenges I have Faced as an Advisor

Here's a quote that I have kept in my briefcase for 35+ years:

"Change has a considerable psychological impact on the human mind. To the fearful it is threatening because it means that things may get worse. To the hopeful it is encouraging because things may get better. To the confident it is inspiring because the challenge exists to make things better."

> **Whitney King, Jr.,** former
> Executive Director of the National
> Urban League (1961) and advisor
> to President Lyndon B. Johnson.

I have seen the following sentence added:

"Obviously then, one's character and frame of mind determine how readily he brings about change and how he reacts to change that is imposed upon him."

7

I am no stranger to serious business transition matters. Here are some examples of some Advisory engagements:

- I worked with a terminally ill business owner who had cancer and no succession plan.
- Another client experienced the sudden diagnosis of a serious disease in one of their children and had to take several months off to take care of her.
- In another case, I worked with a company founder who became disabled and whose spouse was left to operate their multi-million portfolio of business ventures.
- I worked with a relatively healthy owner who was paralyzed by indecision because of a gnawing expansion problem that eventually caused her business to liquidate.
- I have helped a business owner who was two weeks from bankruptcy.
- I managed a partnership split up.
- And I have guided a partnership through dissolution and partial sale of their company when they thought the company had no value.

Each of the above transition point circumstances was accompanied by emotional pain and suffering, confusion, a fogginess of priorities at times, and the negative economic consequences of inaction or incorrect decision-making.

The pain and associated suffering from these unresolved matters and confusion is real. It is at these times that peace of mind becomes priceless. And that peace of mind ironically starts with the paradox of comfort.

The Paradox of Comfort

A paradox means that one thing is true and the opposite is also true. In client business cases I was able to provide options for a way out, around or through a significant transition point (pain). I worked with the clients, with the help of their CPA and legal advisors, and at times key management to acknowledge the reality of the situation. We then agreed upon a plan of action whereby we navigated through the difficulties. From my own business ownership experiences (which I will cover later in the book) I learned invaluable personal lessons about personal suffering and failure. In these moments of intense emotion, I often wanted to escape. But rather, I established a personal practice based on the paradox of comfort. This paradox is powerful in the lesson it teaches:

"Be comfortable with being uncomfortable."

Because of the way we are instinctively wired, we want to fight or flee under threat of fear or pain. By not running from the pain or confusion of my failure, I was able to get through it and shorten the time of suffering. Insights are generally born from our deepest unconscious. It's how I navigate clients to provide options and solutions that are unforeseen by others. I shepherd clients through a foggy, dark and troubling situation and into a process of transformation where they find possibilities, which they had not imagined were available.

**The Paradox of Comfort means standing in there with the emotional pain and allowing it to transform at its pace.
It means the ability to sit with the circumstances,
getting past the discomfort of emotional pain
and confusion, to gain insight.**

It is from these challenging business and personal situations that I have accumulated a great deal of business insight into my practice as a Business Advisor.

The Practice of Business Advice

I look at advising business as a professional practice, like law or medicine. Advisors help business owners solve complex problems. As the business owner's world continues to become more complex, it brings with it more potential for making mistakes on critical decisions that could result in irreversible business meltdowns.

Those of us who engage in the practice of advising therefore bear a great responsibility. The recommendations we make, if implemented, impact lives and livelihoods. This is a personal and professional responsibility, a "duty of care," that I take extremely seriously.

The key to providing effective business advice is insight. Simply defined, insight is the ability to see into and understand the true nature of complex situations. In other words,

Insight is the ability to look past the conventional wisdom and "how we do things here" to see and understand what is *really* going on.

The practice of gaining insight involves the ability to let go of preconceptions and judgments. It requires an ongoing willingness to be wrong about first impressions. Truth must be the highest priority. Insight requires the patience to keep digging into a problem even when one thinks they already know the answer.

When I begin working with a client, the first thing I do is listen intently to what the client and other stakeholders are telling me. The more information I obtain, the better. The next step is to just sit with what I learn, without rushing to judgment. For me, that may involve continued due diligence and further questioning. Sometimes it involves contemplation, meditation, reflection, prayer or sleep. Usually, it involves both. I also may put myself in certain environments to allow the process of insight to work, where I relax and trust that things will get clearer. Soon, I get a feeling of clarity, a "knowingness" that things make sense. The pieces of the puzzle start to unveil a picture and options start to become clear. From insight comes advice.

Advice is the act of making recommendations or providing opinions about what another may do or be faced with. In my work as a Business Advisor, I have eliminated "should" and "could" from their common association with advice. I have replaced that language with "may" and "might." Should and could imply judgment, may and might do not.

Advice carries with it a great responsibility, and therefore the highest value to another is providing *options*, not sole recommendations.

The practice of providing business advice reminds me of a saying I learned in Mergers & Acquisitions (M&A): One buyer is no buyer, meaning that without two buyers vying for the same business, there's no way to keep the value maximized. In terms of advice, I have the following to offer:

One recommendation is no recommendation.

I'm also a seasoned skeptic. I ask questions to understand what I assess, hear, and see is real. I want to make this clear: I don't expect everyone to be convinced that there's more to the business transition experience than what we see, say or do. My instincts and firsthand experiences tell me otherwise. Some may consider my results the work of creativity, luck, or sheer will. Others may call it timing. And still others may call it mere coincidence. To a casual observer, my work may look more ordinary or obvious than special. Some may even shrug and say: So what? And others won't care, which is not uncommon, especially if someone who hasn't faced a crisis or complex business situation.

Each time I tried to verbally explain what occurred in a business transition case, it fled ordinary description. This elusive quality is part of what attracted me to write down my experiences. I was able to uncover what virtues and truths were at work. Writing this book helped me more fully describe what happens in the unseen aspects of giving and receiving business advice. There is much more to it than I initially realized. And by writing it down I became clear on how insight was at work in the process of providing business advice to my clients.

It's profound when we see someone accomplish an almost impossible feat where the odds of success are stacked against them. I've seen it in the lives of those who have confronted extreme difficulty that tests character, limitations, and virtues.

Advice itself has a quality of hope when it is virtuously applied.

My clients have faced such intensely difficult situations and have transcended business-killing conditions. I look back and wonder at what and how that feat was accomplished. Anyone who has initially tried something like golf, tennis, or playing an instrument will recognize that what may seem easy isn't so easy in practice. Making the difficult look easy is the sign of a true professional. And so it is with the practice of providing Business Advice.

The probability exists that the longer someone is in business, a significant difficulty will occur. At the times we need business advice we often do not know where to turn. We're out of ideas, drained from the day-to-day fight, scared, and miserable.

I will be sharing what I have learned so that an owner's journey might be as rewarding. In the context of the giving and receiving of business advice, I will also share some of my more general insights about business and how guiding virtues inform my advisory practice. My intent is that by sharing my journey, it may shine light upon yours.

The Financial Value of Advice

I will begin here with a story.

Who was one of the greatest and most brilliant entrepreneurs in the fast food industry? Most everyone knows the answer: Ray Kroc and his company McDonald's. But very few people know the name of Harry J. Sonneborn.

In 1955, at 52 years old, Ray Kroc was a salesman for MultiMixer, a milkshake equipment manufacturer that supplied restaurants. One day, Ray travelled to San Bernadino, CA to meet his customers,

Maurice "Mac" and Richard McDonald, the owners of a hamburger restaurant. They happened to be using four times the number of milkshake mixers than his average customer. That visit would seal his business destiny.

Kroc was feeling desperate when he made this visit. Hamilton Beach brand mixers were fiercely competing with MultiMixer and his comfortable lifestyle was being jeopardized. He was too old to start over. So when he saw the enthusiasm of the working class families eating at the McDonald's brother's restaurant - burgers, fries, shakes, and pies - he set out to make a deal.

> **INSIGHT:**
> *Influence can be more powerful than impact.*

The deal he made with the McDonald's brothers was to expand their proven restaurant concept. Kroc believed that it could be replicated in other areas of the country. He considered how he would expand and franchising came to mind. A McDonald's franchise would be sold for a low cost of $950 with a 1.9 percent royalty on sales – 1.4 percent to Kroc for overhead and marketing and 0.5 percent for the McDonald's brothers. It was a meager sum for the corporate parent and a far more favorable return to the McDonald's brothers.

Kroc realized later on that he had to confront some serious economic challenges in expanding his company. A large part of the problem Kroc faced was the funding to pay for the land and buildings required for franchise expansion. The corporation's cash flow could only handle one at a time. *"In short, Kroc's concept for building McDonald's was financially bankrupt,"* wrote McDonald's historian John Love in his book, *McDonald's: Behind the Arches* (1995).

That all changed in 1956 when he hired Harry J. Sonneborn, a former Tastee-Freez finance executive, who convinced Kroc that the real money was in real estate. Sonneborn's insight was to have the McDonald's company lease a plot of land and the building for each restaurant. The company would then sublease to the franchisee that would actually run the restaurant. Sonneborn further developed the plan to eventually take out mortgages so that the corporation would own both the building and the land.

Kroc soon established the Franchise Realty Corp. to find willing landowners. *"What converted McDonald's into a money machine had nothing to do with Ray Kroc, or the McDonald brothers, or even the popularity of McDonald's hamburgers, french fries, and milk shakes. It was Harry J. Sonneborn."* (Love, 1995). Just months before Ray Kroc died, he commented: *"Harry alone put in the policy that salvaged this company and made it a big-leaguer. His idea is what made McDonald's rich."* (Love, 1995)

This relatively unknown story of Harry J. Sonneborn and the financial insight he had and advice he shared with Ray Kroc, illustrates clearly the financial value of insight and advice. And those are the kind of insights I want to concentrate on and share with you.

Overview of This Book

This will not be your typical business book. Over the course of the following pages, I will be telling stories, discussing some of my own ideas, and sharing some of what I have learned from others. I will bounce from my business experience to my own personal growth and to guiding virtues from wise mentors. I will go off on tangents and occasional rants.

CHAPTER 1: INTRODUCTION

My friend and colleague Bob Everett has helped me get this book into shape. Bob has been a business professor (University of Maryland, Johns Hopkins), an entrepreneur, and a consultant. He has helped me to understand and organize what I have learned over a 35+ year career. He has also helped link many of my thoughts and experiences into the broader base of business literature.

I begin the book with a brief autobiography showing how I came to learn what I know and believe what I believe. I share my experience with mentors that helped me on my zigzag quest of entrepreneur, professional manager, and advisor. This is followed by a chapter on why business owners seek advice, informal and formal networks for advice and the reasons why owners may seek and resist advice.

The subsequent chapters address the scientific basis for business advice with excerpts from neuroscience and psychology, the transition points in business when advice matters most, and the critical role outside advice plays in the practice of business ownership. I will cover the ways in which advice is killed, adopted, or rejected in the next chapters. And I will conclude with what I consider to be the guiding virtues that provide the fertile ground for obtaining insight and providing advice.

I have laid out the final two chapters for those who may be interested in becoming a professional advisor, mostly because I believe there is a significant value in this practice of advice. Then I close with reflections on insight and advice and a final overview. Basically, I am including here many ideas that I wanted to include earlier, but could not find a suitable place for them.

As a matter of reference, I will be using third person of he and she, his and her alternatively throughout the book when referring to an owner. A business owner will be referenced as singular owner or plural owner(s). My description of a business owner is: the primary shareholder in a privately-held business who has the authority to make the ultimate operating decisions regarding business matters and is responsible to others for making a profit. The owner description for purposes of this book include the managing partner, managing member, managing director, and managing principal in partnerships and LLC's.

The hardest part of this whole project has been finding a way to organize it in a way that makes sense. Books, by their very nature, are linear. One word follows another until you get to the end. However, our human brains do not work that way. We bounce around internally from idea to idea, like mental butterflies, until we land on something that seems to work. Thoughts, concepts, memories, linkages, inferences, intuitions, imaginations, confusions, and conclusions ebb and flow in a continuous internal rhythm of "ripples and waves." It's how we think and how we learn. It's our unique strength as conscious beings. Therefore, I have put the minimum organization I thought necessary to capture the essence of my thoughts. I want to let you, the reader, engage in what I have to say.

The thoughts I present in this book have been learned from experience, from gifted teachers, and through my connection with my spiritual self.

The occasionally uncomfortable journey has been worth it, often in surprising and delightful ways. Today, I have an abundant business advisory practice and a comfortable income as long as I want to work. I have the respect of my colleagues and my clients. Most of them I can honestly call friends.

I believe it is both more powerful and more joyous to live our lives, personal, professional, and spiritual, as part of a single whole, bringing the experiences and resources from each to enhance and inform the others. Then we can truly and powerfully put ourselves in service to others, reaping the personal, spiritual, and, yes, the financial rewards earned by doing so.

I am fortunate to have the love of my wife of over thirty-eight years and I am close to all four of my children. I have the blessings of six grandchildren. My parents and in-laws have been proud supporters of my life's calling in business. My younger brother Dan and two younger sisters Brenda and Beth and I talk frequently and end conversations with "Love you." to another, and we mean it. I have a few close friends who know me well. I have a variety of outdoor interests that keep me grounded. And, perhaps most importantly, I curiously find that I understand what I bring to this world and I am at peace.

This is what I wish for you.

❖　❖　❖

Chapter 2: The Blessings of an Ordinary Life

❖ ❖ ❖

An Ordinary Life

Before I expect you to believe what I am saying in this book, I think it is important that you know where I came from and how I have learned what I now know and how I have developed some measure of insight along the way.

At age 23, I literally risked everything I owned and invested in myself by starting my first business. Since then I have invested my life working hard to earn a living and I make a good living on a consistent basis. I have sometimes chased the wrong dreams and caught them; not realizing until later the wrong dreams were preparation for living the right dream. I have tried to make sense of my personal struggles in life and to understand the suffering of others. I still believe in priorities - God, family, work, and friends - and in the values of service and stewardship. I learned early in life to be a provider and protector, before a playmate. I believe that a measure of a person is how one keeps their promises, especially to themself. I am an ordinary guy who for the last 35+ years has been a student of business and people, and believes at this point in his life, that he has something to say.

Central to my life as a youth and adolescent was growing up in the City of Lancaster, Pennsylvania attending Sacred Heart Parochial School and Sacred Heart Catholic Church. They were a half block away from my home. I served as an altar boy for weddings, funerals, regular weekly services, holidays and holy days of obligation. I also enjoyed service work for the clergy, performing landscaping and general cleanup duties at the convent and rectory. I would eventually start mowing lawns as a summer job and then worked part-time as a busboy at the Rea & Derrick restaurant counter. School, service, and work gave me a break from the pressures of city life. We eventually moved in 1969 to the suburbs of Lancaster, Manheim Township when I enrolled in Lancaster Catholic High School.

At the same time, it seemed like my external and internal worlds were in transition at once. Change was being thrust upon our nation with the civil rights movement, a prolonged war in the jungles of South Vietnam, political scandals, Woodstock, the music of Jimi Hendrix, The Rolling Stones, The Doors, Led Zeppelin and Vatican II in the Catholic Church. There were more questions being asked than answers provided. It felt like every aspect of life was blanketed with major voices of change, creating uncertainty and upheaval of the established status quo. On the threshold of adolescence my world had gone from structured to crazy and out-of-control. And the electricity in world events fascinated me.

During high school I was active in football and wrestling where I honed a deep-rooted competitive spirit. If football summer practice didn't kill us, I imagined I could survive almost anything. It was our coach's personal form of the Marine Corps Crucible. Upon graduation I attended Bloomsburg State College and wrestled in the Huskies Division I program. Athletics taught me to fear no man, but respect all. After two years I decided that my education was more important than athletics and enrolled for my final two years at Millersville State College. At the end of the summer of 1975 I married my high school sweetheart, Toni (Arcudi) Wimer. In 1977, I graduated from Millersville with a Bachelor of Arts in Psychology.

We were expecting our first child in July 1977. And I was having classic panic attacks while reading the newspapers for job openings. My Uncle Fred was a salesman so I figured I would pursue those opportunities. He had had a tremendous amount of freedom as a salesperson to work his hours. Sales sounded like something I might find interesting. Fortunately my search efforts with an employment agency resulted in employment as a salesman with 3M Company selling copiers. My career had begun. I was proud of my start and relieved that I had landed. It would be the start of my practical education in business.

The Four Mentors

I am fortunate to have four primary mentors who have been with me most of my life: Fred, Dad, Gene, and Jeff. Each of these men helped me to learn, grow, and develop in different ways. And to them I attribute certain character traits that I outline in Chapter 9 as Guiding Virtues. They weren't the only people who had impact and influence on me. My grandfather's Bill and Clarence, grandmothers Catherine and Mildred and my Aunt Matilda each had a significant influence on who I became in my youth and through adulthood.

I've also had athletic coaches and educators who were unusually dedicated and caring people. Likewise, I had some who were unbelievably incompetent. I learned much from both, and sometimes more from the worst. It's equally important to decide who you *do not* want to become. The Four Mentors happened to be sent to me as gifted teachers to counsel me and prepare me on this advisory way of life.

Fred: The Outdoorsman

In the early part of my growing up, my father was very busy going to night school in addition to building his very successful career at Armstrong World Industries. As the oldest of four children, I was basically on my own as my mother handled the household and my three younger siblings. I was eleven when my mother's brother Fred showed interest in taking me hunting and fishing. He was a Metropolitan Insurance salesman and Air Force veteran.

Fred had a life-long passion for the outdoors, especially hunting and fishing. He taught me to handle both a fly rod and a firearm with precision and respect. It was Fred that lit my spirit of adventure and exploration, and it was Fred that taught me a reverence for life and respect for the wilderness.

Our outdoor journeys sparked in me a flame of curiosity about life and nature. We could stand in wonder and awe at the beauty and ferocity of nature and remark at how lucky we were to be alive. Fred was someone I could count on regardless of what else was going on in my life or his. Our friendship was built on an unspoken mutual trust. We had one another's back. We are eternally bound by our outdoor adventures. I can still hear his affectionate voice echo in my mind as he called me "Davey." Fred was my guide for learning what was important in grounding me in life. I found a sanctuary in nature that rekindles joy, wonder, awe and awareness of my own nature and being. When I become distracted, and sometimes off course on my internal compass, I still go to the deep woods and reflect. For me, it just works.

Fred would teach me lessons of living an authentic life regardless of what others thought or said. He would also eventually teach me about pursuing what you love, about the natural consequences in life, and the dignity of death. Fred taught me the Guiding Virtues of Adaptability, Compassion and Curiosity.

Dad: The Financial Chief

As a young man I learned a lot about business from my father at our kitchen table where he would work late each evening. The older I got, the more I appreciated his practical form of financial wisdom and business insight. By the time I was in business for myself, he was my primary source of external business guidance.

With every new business venture, I always looked to him for advice. He was a role model for me. I would congratulate him on his accomplishments. I was proud of him. I also believe I inherited a genetic, sixth sense for numbers from him. I still can't figure out how he led such a full life. He raised four children. He was a loving father, devoted husband to my mother Janet, a career-minded executive, who attended night school for nine years to obtain an undergraduate degree. He was a man who counted Sunday Offerings after Mass, was a Knight of Columbus and managed to retire with a pension after 42 years of service to the same company.

23

This all was quite remarkable for a man from ordinary circumstances. For example, he and my mother would tell me about how they cleaned apartments to subsidize their rent. They would save change to buy ice cream to share. I cannot think of a better way to enjoy small change.

Dad eventually reached the executive suite with uncommon success and integrity. He'd often say that he didn't belong to the country club so he could maintain his objectivity. He was always available and I never took that for granted. I was grateful that Dad never judged me or my pursuits, although we could agree to disagree. I felt he was always available for decision support and would only offer advice if asked. He was certainly patient in many ways.

One time he clarified something for me when I was procrastinating about making an operating decision. I asked Dad what his decision would be if he were President. He reminded me, *"Dave, it's not my job to make decisions about the direction of the company. I have input. And I provide options. I can voice my opinion. But final decisions are made by the CEO, whether or not I like them."* That humble explanation helped me understand his perspective from experience and clarified my role. Most importantly, I was left to make the business decision alone. Later, in my life as an Advisor, I understood his lesson much more clearly. Dad taught me the Guiding Virtues of Accountability, Humility, and Integrity.

Gene: The Entrepreneur

At 3M, I met Gene, my new Sales Manager. I needed to work at learning how to sell as I was a naturally introverted person.

Gene was a naturally gifted "people person." He was a tough act to match. Sales helped me learn about people and their behaviors. It also allowed me to learn more about my own strengths and weaknesses. I learned that street smarts, drive, and determination overcame many of my deficiencies and natural introversion. I'd learn later that many of the best sales professionals were actually introverted and not "born." Introverts may have ended up selling less volume, but their sales would result in long-term customers and excellent referrals. More of their sales would stick and they would have better margins. Introverts paid attention to the details. I prescribed to that path especially in learning how to be a better communicator.

Most times I succeeded in a sale with persistence, product knowledge, and outworking the competition. During cold calls, I developed an outward selling style that overcame inner anxieties. I leaned on my past athletic experiences to push through questions of self-confidence. I took on competitive situations with intensity and vigor. I had the spirit to compete firmly ingrained in me. Many lessons from those two and a half years of early on-the-job sales experiences would mold me for a lifetime of business dealings. I became quite resourceful from those lessons in sales.

When Gene left 3M for an entrepreneurial venture, I decided it would soon be time for me to leave 3M as well. After Gene's first venture failed in 1978, he and I each borrowed from a Bank, leveraged our assets and started a business together: Eugene Davids Co. We used our first names because we figured it would exemplify our commitment to personal relationships with our customers. It was a business partnership that would last eighteen years.

Over that time, my entrepreneurial itch and my developing sense of business as an adventure led to the launching of an additional five start-ups in diverse businesses. These were also fueled by Gene's and my desires to keep something new percolating while working at our core business. These businesses were all related to our core office products business and included an office furniture business and a fax dealership. During this time I learned the value of having a partner and sharing the demands of business. The work was fun and challenging and the times were mostly good.

Gene was the biggest influence in developing my early, raw people skills and salesmanship. He had been my manager and mentor, and now was my partner. My father served as an informal business advisor to us during many of those years. Dad, Gene, and I would talk about various business situations whenever we met. As a life-long bachelor, Gene had dedicated himself to his career and taking care of his mother. So his work was his life. And I have always respected him for his ability to connect with people at any level of an organization. Gene taught me the Guiding Virtues of Connectedness, Passion, and Resourcefulness.

Jeff: The Merlin

Hardships – real or imagined – arrive at every business doorstep. It's a phenomenon of being in business. At several points between 1978 and 1996, our financial results at the company were being impacted by lackluster sales or a recession. We needed to tighten our operation and constantly strove to keep our costs down. And that ongoing cost pressure caused us major stress internally.

Since Gene and I both believed that people were a critical piece of our success, we engaged a business coaching firm to work with us on hiring, selection and placing people in positions where they would tap their strengths. It occurred to me that I could also use someone independent as an executive sounding board to sort through things that were gnawing at me, both personal and professional. That was when I met Jeff, a clinical psychologist and business coach.

I felt there were some blockages that I couldn't break through alone and having an independent, objective person who was qualified to help me sort things out made sense. One blockage was that, in my late 30's, I still did not have a broad enough role model for being President of a company. My father was excellent in finance, Gene was excellent in sales. I needed someone to help me be the generalist I knew I needed to be. The other blockage was my self-generated competition with my father. He was a big man in a big company. I was a big man too, but in a very small company. I didn't think I measured up.

I searched for some time to find a fit with a peer group, but nothing really excited me. What I wanted was deeper work to get to my core business strengths and to see myself from a different perspective. So I engaged Jeff as my business performance coach with a two-year plan to focus on my growth and professional development as a manager and a leader. It happened to be a time where my Dad was being promoted often for his ability to solve problems on an international scale. And our business was floundering. So the timing was ripe to reach out for help to work through personal matters as well.

Jeff helped me with both of my major blockages. He and I discussed my turmoil surrounding Dad. For some reason I had felt like I was always competing with him. What became clear in talking with Jeff was that my perspective was limited. I had been comparing and trying to live up to the standards my father set for his own world. It's all I had known as my role model to emulate in business. Jeff asked me, *"Dave, did you ever consider that your father could not be as big a king in your kingdom of owning a privately-held business?"* Wow! That made sense. I could never be as big a king as he was in his kingdom – the corporate world, but he couldn't do what I was doing either. That perspective immediately resonated. Suddenly the weight on my shoulders lifted. I resolved years of self-doubt and self-pressure. It now made sense. Dad was simply living his life doing work he loved for a corporation he respected. And I had chosen a different path altogether.

When I told my Dad the story of how I was feeling, he admitted that he had sensed edginess from me. He said he had never felt that way about me or held any expectations other than that I was happy. I explained that I had actually been wrestling with it for many years. It felt deeply emotional and I was bottled up inside. And that I finally needed to understand what was bothering me so I sought independent advice. I explained that with the help of a trusted performance coach, I had identified the root cause of my feelings. I felt I was not measuring up, no matter how hard I worked. After that conversation with Dad, I resolved years of self-pressure and the issue reconciled for me.

In the course of my professional development, Jeff would play a key role introducing me to my strengths. Jeff didn't hold back and I was a willing student. He taught me how to be introspective and mindful. He recommended courses in self-development that touched my soul. I read voraciously. Soon, through diligent practice, I was seeing things differently and my life began to change. It took time, but once I had incorporated the lessons, my perspective grew regarding the business.

It would become a process that would change how I saw the world and how I saw myself in business.

Jeff had taught me to learn from the messages in my pain, rather than to run from my pain.

And now I was ready for my next challenge as a solo business owner. Jeff taught me the Guiding Virtues of Acceptance, Contemplation, Intuition and Patience.

The Path of Entrepreneur

The company Gene and I had built was moving along steadily, but I was growing more discontented. After four years incubating a new software integration and technology line of business, it became evident to me that as partners Gene and I had grown in different ways. I was also feeling not so good about my personal development as a business owner. I wanted more stimulation in management know-how. I was feeling boxed in, unhappy, stymied, and stagnant.

After addressing my thoughts and feelings with Gene over some period of time, we agreed to separate the businesses. After eighteen years and five successful start-ups we split amicably, at least on the surface. At this time, we were only operating two businesses: the office products and a software development company. The others had been closed or sold. Gene took the main part of the core business: office products. I took the riskier technology group and a multi-year buyout. I finally had my own ship to captain.

We had enjoyed the perfect complement of skills. Many who knew us as partners thought of us as Mr. Inside and Mr. Outside. Looking back, I can understand that perspective. However, I wanted and needed more of something that, at the time, I could not put my finger on.

Both of us carried some guilt for many years about the divestiture. Gene did not really understand why I needed to leave the business. I eventually explained to him that I had a deep need to lead and guide my own ship. I no longer wanted to be held in the shadows of my older, superstar sales partner. Over time, he finally understood. And that made sense enough for both of us to heal the remaining issues between us.

Eating Humble Pie

Little did I know at the time that my short entrepreneurial debut in business was about to change dramatically. In late 1997 while the technology business was at its peak of 25 people, I began to see that the threat of Y2K was having an impact on forecasted project work for the large-scale electronic document management software development and systems integration services my company was providing. The business had invested heavily in technical labor to see through a $1.8 million project at a Mid-western nuclear plant. This job had the potential for huge profits and was to be the start of many such projects.

> **INSIGHT:**
> *Sometimes, things go right for all the wrong reasons, and wrong for all the right reasons.*

It was a case of doing all the right things, but having the outcome result in a financial disaster. For reasons having nothing to do with us, water cooling towers began to freeze up at the nuclear generating plant that was our customer. The Nuclear Regulatory Commission consequently shut down the plant in order to ensure the stability of the reactors. Meanwhile, our technology project remained unfunded even after a pilot run had proven its economic value. After the NRC intervention, all deployable assets at the nuclear facility were redirected by the plant owner to the reactor cooling issues.

By early 1998 it was too late to re-balance direction and re-organize efforts. My prized newly divested business took two financial punches – Y2K delaying technology investments and an unanticipated nuclear plant shutdown. We didn't have the capital to bridge the delays or contract loss. We were overleveraged and in six months, we became a two-punch KO capital casualty. And my personal life was about to get worse.

Bearing the full weight of the business crisis, I became depressed and lost – an ego-shattering event. Questions arose in my mind over and over again. How could this happen? I became distracted and angry.

On the personal side, I had not talked with my wife Toni about the critical state of the business until the last minute. This was for a number of reasons. Foremost in my mind was that she could not help me fix it. But at the time, I hadn't considered that I needed her emotional support, but was too proud to ask. It was a decision I regretted later as it affected our relationship. She felt betrayed and isolated. I felt more isolated and even questioned the foundation of our life as a married couple.

I needed time to heal and wanted to get away to think. I felt cornered by circumstances and carried a terrible sense of guilt and fear about what others thought of me. I moved out of our home for six months to regain my sense of self. Toni and I both felt the devastation of losing the relatively new endeavor, which had been going so well. Now our entire family felt a pain of separation due to things that were beyond our control. I knew I needed to prioritize and put together the shattered pieces of my personal life, my family, and my entrepreneurial life.

I wondered if the embarrassment of a business failure would ever go away. I questioned myself incessantly. I realized I needed to learn some new skills. So I jumped back on the path of accountability, tightened my belt and made a commitment to work at rebuilding my life.

Sometimes, in the darkness of life's most devastating moments, all things are made possible. And so my lesson in eating humble pie oddly delivered the gift of gratitude.

My pain (failure) carried with it a message (an insight). Instead of running from it or denying it, I chose to confront it and acknowledge it. Avoidance or denial of pain is what drives other things to go haywire and intensify like addictions and obsessive behaviors and on and on. Rather, the healthy answer was simple: Deal with it. By settling in, confronting the matter and acknowledging the pain, I stopped feeling bad about having it. And I was able to concentrate on the solutions and options for the problem at hand.

What became clear to me in the insights were:

1. What I really, really wanted, and
2. What, if any was the real fear or impending negative consequence, and not just my vivid imagination, and
3. What the next steps could be in terms of possibilities

And so the lesson of being comfortable with being uncomfortable had started to unveil. It was now time to apply my lesson in other business owner's settings as a professional manager.

The Path of Professional Manager

After my decision to move back home, my life got back on a positive track. For the next six years, I leveraged what I had learned and became an in-house turnaround executive and change leader. I would transform from being a business owner and captain of my own ship to being a professional manager for another owner.

Looking back, opportunities just showed up. After a successful ERP technology recovery engagement with a manufacturer, I was rewarded with a full-time executive position as the COO of a $20MM manufacturing plant with two Fortune 500 customers. I accepted the challenge. That led to another COO position in a turnaround of a $110MM manufacturing plant that resulted in a sale of the multi-generational business to its NYSE-traded largest customer. And then a $400MM conglomerate had a $12MM subsidiary that needed leadership to make changes in both sales and costs at the same time.

I could not have planned events this way. They just happened. I knew I wanted to learn more about finance and my life rewarded this intention.

Each challenge sharpened my skills in finding new ways out of problems or around obstacles. I started to provide unforeseen options and solutions. And the people and businesses responded. Everyone knew their role and received feedback consistently. We met as equals. We built trust in one another. I always had more questions for them than answers, but I noticed if I asked the right questions, they generally had the right answers. The process was working and now I recognized it. Progress was being made on many fronts.

Reflecting on these successes, I also recognized some paradoxes. Going into each executive assignment, I did not have a pre-conceived idea of what to do to solve the problem.

It was an unconventional approach because in all cases, I replaced someone who had deep industry knowledge.

In fact, my value to the owner(s) was that I did not have industry blinders. By taking a completely fresh look at the situation and by listening to the team, I had managed to take the same team members generally that had been previously floundering and bind them by a common cause. Together, we found the way out. The successes were remarkable.

We beat the odds in every case. No one had done it before me in any of these situations. The outcomes weren't statistically pre-dictable. But applying my methodology at the outset resulted in positive outcomes. I knew I was on to something but I didn't quite under-stand it nor did I have the time to organize it. I was too busy applying myself to new business challenges. It was if I had been handed the answer to my incessant questions about my own business ownership tragedy. What did it take to change from an under-performing state to a performing one? My only answer I received at the time aired on a commercial – *"Just do it."* And that's what I did.

> **INSIGHT:**
> *Miracles in business occur quietly for keen observers to celebrate.*

Each of these turnaround situations was emotionally taxing and nearly miraculous in the way it turned out. It was not an easy or comfortable road, especially when I did something the owners didn't understand. It was their company and their anxiety was high. In the end, they were the ones who had to live with the results, so they often felt a need to do things their way. As the senior executive(s), we had to negotiate actions all along the way. This prolonged the misery at times, but we took the time to develop mutual understanding and get things right. I relied on common sense and practical experience to shepherd changes. Then, the team did the work. I supported their decisions. They got the credit. I encouraged them to experiment and come up with problem solutions on their own. Team members grew and developed as leaders. After a while, I found I was no longer needed and could move on to the next challenge.

Independence and consulting looked appealing to me again. I had been cautious in allowing those thoughts to rekindle, especially after the loss of my technology business. I knew I had crossed an unusual chasm from entrepreneur to professional manager. It took me six years. With my newly developed skills and confidence I wanted to reenter the world of business ownership.

Again, my desires were answered. In April 2005 I had a consulting client in the moving business who was interested in a turnaround when she decided to dissolve the business. She had received a lucrative position in a larger organization and was looking forward to a position with less stress than she was experiencing as a business owner. Her current company had a new logistics contract opportunity she needed either to transfer or cancel and she was concerned about contract termination, her legal liabilities and potential liquidated damages.

I assessed the opportunity and challenges for myself. In the end, I accepted the contract and, in the space of four weeks, started up a multi-state, last-mile delivery company for custom kitchen cabinetry. At the same time I was feeling bullish economically and funded my son-in-law in an auto repair franchise where I would be the silent financial partner and he would operate it. I felt calm knowing I was applying my newly developed skills and experiences.

God must have had a sense of humor watching me put these two deals together, quite possibly for all the wrong reasons. Because what I thought I would be doing for that year was entirely different than what happened next.

The Epiphany of Primary Care

There's nothing that hits you in the gut worse than a child's illness, especially cancer. Three weeks after my two start-ups in April 2005 my middle daughter was suddenly diagnosed with non-Hodgkin's lymphoma. In an instant my world as I knew it started coming apart at the seams.

Our family was raw with pain from the news and anxious to get something done. Several well-known cancer hospitals had a 3-4 weeks wait before she could be treated. We couldn't wait. And then an unexpected gift arrived. I received a call from a clinical trial analyst in response to an email I sent about her case to a general info@ email address. Johns Hopkins had elected to include her in one of their clinical trials and we needed to report to the hospital in 24 hours. I consider that email a miracle in our lives.

During her chemotherapy I volunteered as her primary care-giver and committed to her schedule of chemo every third weekend. Subsequently, I turned over my business to a capable former colleague and concentrated on learning what living with cancer and survivor-ship were all about. After her chemotherapy protocol proved only 90% effective for eliminating my daughter's disease, the medical pro-fessionals explained that the softball sized mass in her chest would return aggressively. The doctors recommended a stem cell trans-plant. It was a grueling 35 days in John Hopkins Hospital. Somehow God was making sure I was there in her darkest days. On the bright days she had visits from her husband, her 9-month old son and other family members. I just surrendered to the fact that I still had more to learn.

I found quiet spaces in my new surroundings of the Kimmel Cancer Center and Johns Hopkins Main Buildings. I had time on my hands when I could reflect on what I had been doing and what I was going to be doing. Work looked a heck of a lot easier to me than fight-ing this disease. It was during these times of quiet contemplation that I made a promise to myself. I knew my emotional reservoir was being depleted by care giving. But I questioned the reasons I had said yes to operating the two businesses. What did I really, really want out of my work life?

The insights started to build and crest.

In order to re-energize, I needed to let go of a stressor.
My priorities had come in conflict with my desires.

And it came to me in an epiphany what I needed to do with my work. The logistics business was sold at the end of 2005 and I didn't look back. I also sold my interest in the franchise with my son-in-law. I wanted freedom to not be shackled to any one business.

Today my daughter is eight years in remission. It took her faith, love of family, love for her son and the loving, intelligent care of the medical community and science technology at Johns Hopkins to heal. And my life changed because of her illness. I made a pact with myself to do the work I loved as if it was my last month I had on earth. My last seven years of advisory work and this book are the outcomes of my journey.

The Path of Advisor

Since 2006, I have advised numerous business owners, applying many hands-on, sleeves rolled up experiences to solve complex problems and take advantage of unrecognized and unexpected opportunities. The results have been remarkable. In fact some results are just short of miraculous.

I've been fortunate to have met some extraordinary people who had done nothing to deserve the personal or business circumstances in which they found themselves.

- I've confronted business situations of owners with sudden and severe medical issues.
- I've worked through serious estate, competency, and legal matters.
- I've worked with business crisis and business creativity in the same assignment.
- I've worked closely with spouses of owners and multi-generation family members, who had to take over running a family business

about which they initially knew little. Over time, I helped them develop the confidence and security to make exceptional decisions about their businesses without the founder.

- I have saved my clients millions in potentially lost value and cash flow.

My value is an ability to provide key decision support, strategic insight, and clarity on issues.

When life presents the unexpected (as it often does), I provide options and potential pathways through it. When I am able to work with an owner to prepare and plan for transitions, many of the potential negative consequences can be avoided.

In the past, I had wondered how much of a demand was really out there for business advice. What I have found is that the problems are there and are increasingly complex. Some are apparent. Some are not so apparent. Many of these problems are hidden from the owner and do not become apparent until they actually threaten the survival of the business. And so I wondered how I might help. What was it that I could do to make a difference in another business owner's life?

As owners we can go it alone and suffer the vagaries of isolation while remaining "inside the box." Or we can look in the mirror and acknowledge that we do not and cannot know everything. We all could use some help at times to ease the burden.

I have found that the solution to a complex problem is more about relying on the strengths of people than it is about trying to change their weaknesses.

39

Today, I advise, teach and speak on the topic of business insight to those who feel these lessons are valuable.

- I guide owners in the preparation of their business for sale or succession or other transition to new management.
- I concentrate on preserving and maximizing the value of the business.
- I also navigate clients through the complexities of major business change and transformation: ownership crisis, turn-around, acquisition, dissolution, reorganization, debt restructure, and/or joint venture.
- I regularly engage with other professionals, attorneys, and CPA's advising the owner to shape the most effective solutions to strategic and financial situations.
- And I rigorously maintain confidentiality in every aspect of what I do.

We are each dealt a hand of cards. We just need to figure out how to play the hand we're dealt. It takes the willingness to show up, take risks, be willing to fail, act decisively, and be accountable for the results. It takes the courage to work through the fear that looms large in our minds. These lessons cannot be learned in a classroom. They cannot be handed to you by your parents. They must be learned through struggle, effort, and humility in the arena of business.

These are blessings of an ordinary life.

❖   ❖   ❖

Chapter 3: Why Owners Seek Advice

❖   ❖   ❖

Introduction

The activity of giving and receiving advice is an integral part of business life.

Most business owners are always seeking some kind of advice because of either their natural curiosity to learn or because they are facing a situation that they have never experienced before.

It may not appear to them that they are asking, but it's still true. In order to *stay* in business, owners must develop sophisticated radar for anticipating events. It's a natural process that evolves over time. Whether or not they pay attention to this radar is another story.

My point is that owners stay in business by figuring out their competitive world in some way. In most cases, the owner seeks advice because something has triggered them out of their comfort zone. It's described as "red flags went up," or something "hit their radar," or they just "don't feel right." In this book, I refer to such events as "Transition Points."

We know that owners generally understand that they aren't islands. They cannot rely solely on their own counsel.

Transition Points for Advice

Usually, owners rely on their informal and formal networks for most of their advice needs. Unfortunately, few business owners recognize the value of a professional, outside Business Advisor until some crisis happens. This is called a "triggering event." This is the one event, big or small, that finally convinces the owner that they can no longer do everything themselves and that they need some serious help.

> **INSIGHT:**
> *Time is an enemy and an ally of every leader.*

These events can take many different forms: being put on a "watch list" by the bank, the loss of one too many customers to a competitor, a cash flow crisis, a lawsuit, or the sudden illness of the owner. In our experience, these triggering events are of four basic types:

1. **An unforeseen event or "Black Swan"**
   This can be internal (a fire in the building or the incapacitation of the owner) or external (the introduction of a game changing technology by a competitor or a drastic change in government regulatory requirements). The important thing here is that the event was difficult or impossible to predict, yet must be dealt with immediately.

2. **A bad business decision**
   Anyone who has ever run a company knows that you can't get it right every time. That new product idea or new location that looked so promising, the acquisition that would take the

business to the next level, or that new Operations VP with the excellent resume may seem like great ideas at the time but create severe problems later on.

3. **Too Much, Too Fast**
   Sometimes a business, especially in its early stages, can be "too" successful. It takes on too many customers, too many new projects, too many new people, and too much debt. The business cannot keep up with the cash flow. The P&L may even show profits, but the payroll cannot be met.

4. **Automatic Pilot**
   This is another problem that can be born of success and is probably the most common problem I see. Businesses continue to do the things that made them initially successful even after circumstances have changed. It may even take months or years before this problem turns into a crisis. The paradox here is that sometimes after problems start to arise, owners want to "go back to basics." In other words, they insist on continuing the practices that created the problem in the first place, or that address problems of the past rather than problems of the present or future.

In most crisis situations, the triggering event reveals levels of complexity and creates emotional burdens that make it very difficult for the owner, sitting in the middle of the situation, to figure out exactly what needs to be done.

**He may spend days in crisis management or "firefighting"
rather than taking the time to look at the big picture.**

The mindset becomes one of fear and extremes rather than confidence and taking prudent action.

When the transition point is finally recognized, there are usually no easy cause & effect restorative solutions. The immediate fix, "silver bullet," or instant answer often throws the problem into overdrive, especially if the owner has made promises regarding problem solutions. The return to financial recovery and operating normalcy may be a long road to travel. The emotional toll to the owner can be devastating as she gets into this circular bind:

**The worse she feels, the less well she thinks; and
the less well she thinks, the worse she feels.**

In high growth situations, the owner usually has a clear vision of where the business is headed and the business may be growing at a phenomenal rate. What often causes the triggering event is "speed and greed." The business tries to capture markets or market share in a short window of opportunity in order to acquire market leadership and dominance.

**In this high growth mode processes are stressed, broken,
or unable to keep up. People are frenzied and roles
are mismatched.**

Yet, in spite of its organizational problems and lack of profits, the business may continue to grow from the love and passion of the founder and/or the demands of its customers. Capital can become exhausted and the business can be cash-poor and at risk of failure. In this environment, service may suffer, customer relationships may become stressed, and employees may become disillusioned. Decisions are made primarily with growth in mind and the potential for future problems is discounted or ignored.

Finally, there is the "stuff-that-happens" situation. Circumstances may change overnight due to an owner's injury or illness, a family member's untimely death, an unplanned disability, a divorce, an accident, or any number of other personal situations.

**Simultaneously dealing with both business demands
and high personal demands may become
overwhelming for the owner.**

This is a time where an interim leader may serve the owner well until the demands level out.

Take for instance a spouse or heir suddenly left with a business they do not know how to run. Some very profitable businesses lose their momentum from these life events. Some businesses are not prepared for a succession, much less from an unexpected inheritance. The question for the new owner becomes, "What do we do now?" Left to chance and without an experienced executive in charge, the business starts to drift off course and lose its direction.

> **INSIGHT:**
> *The complex can be made simple if we only allow it.*

Immediate care must be given to the big picture as the complexities of the business roll on. Quite often CPA's and corporate counsel are aware of these situations. However, I find that very few, if any of these professionals, are prepared to "clear the decks," to step in and guide the company's leadership or operations during the turmoil. This is what a Business Advisor is skilled to do.

Regardless of the cause or type, these triggering events will kick owners out of their comfort zone. Owners now have three basic choices:

1. They can retreat back into that comfort zone and try to weather the storm (the "hope" strategy) going it alone,
2. They can "wing it" on their own or,
3. They can get some professional help to navigate the events

Benefits of Advice

The benefits of having professional guidance during these triggering events almost always outweigh the investment required. Generally when there is a critical issue facing the business, there are also grave financial consequences. The business must either take action to avert the consequences of the crisis or just push through it. The value of the Business Advisor at these times is quite clear. The right Advisor will have travelled similar waters.

- **The Advisor will understand the dynamics of what's at stake and will help to calculate the economic and emotional risks of alternative actions.** Having new options where once none seemed available can be very comforting.

- **Additionally, the right Advisor helps to provide options that the owner may never have considered.** In other words, the Advisor provides another set of eyes on the problem and is able to take a fresh, unbiased look. Based on the Advisor's experiences with other businesses, there may be new perspectives that can be applied to the problem.

In one case, a client told me she was worried about her cash flow. It was short by ten thousand dollars per month. She asked why I didn't seem as upset by that situation as she was. I replied that I had worked my way out of being short one million per week in cash flow, so in comparison I believed we could work our way through the situation.

- **Perspective is a valuable asset during any crisis.** Sometimes the problem may not be as large or ugly as it first seems.

Being open and unbiased does not mean that the Advisor doesn't know anything about the business. In fact, many times, knowing less detail about *how* the business works allows the Advisor to make recommendations to solve the bigger problems facing the business. In fact, what the owner may see as a problem, the Advisor may see as an opportunity or benefit.

During ownership transitions,

- **Advisors can assume the role of consultant and act in the role of a project manager during the transition journey.** In this role, the Advisor is a special assistant to the CEO. The Advisor interacts with the key management team to outline the steps of the transition. The Advisor gains alignment between the team members and chief executive. It is this ability to collaborate on critical change objectives and to measure progress that provides value to the owner and the business.

In the role of Facilitator,

- **The Advisor becomes a teacher as well to the key management team members.** As action items are met and the facilitated team grows in confidence, performance results can be used as a scorecard tracking the successful progress of the transition effort.

The bottom line is that the Advisor,

- **Can become the primary catalyst for making the changes necessary in the business.** Along that journey, the Advisor may fill the roles of teacher, coach and mentor.

So with all these benefits of engaging an Advisor, why do owners wait so long to do so or refuse to entirely? Knowing why helps us understand and appreciate the owner's dilemma and how Advisors might overcome their resistance.

Informal Networks

The first place a typical owner goes to for advice is their informal network. Informal networks may include:

- Spouse or Significant Other
- Another Family Member
- Key Employee or Partner
- Business Colleague
- The "Buddy" System

Informal networks are usually convenient and readily accessible. They are so integrated into work life that they do not really get noticed. They just happen naturally. Generally these informal networks provide the owner with an opportunity to discuss problems and bounce ideas and concepts off of friends they trust. However, what is cautionary is that owner subjectivity may preclude making any real progress. Generally there's no accountability. And the informal network knows the owner in a certain setting, so there may be concern for letting her guard down, especially because of knowing them socially.

Informal networks have a natural, built-in subjectivity. The question for the owner is this: Can you actually get to the hard truth, or do you have to put on an appearance? Conversely, does the informal network feel a need to protect you or shield you from the hard truth? Do they become so subjective that they can't see the hard truth, themselves?

Each of the above informal sources for advice also has a tradeoff. Confidentiality cannot always be assured and, when relationships are important, total honesty may be hard to come by, depending upon the topic.

Quite typically, the owner utilizes these sources for casual talk and poking at some of the daily matters that may be percolating. In particular, the close friend "Buddy" model may include a regular time where the owner can relax and talk while enjoying an activity with golf, tennis, fishing, or hunting partners in an unrelated field. Business problems are discussed in the same way, and usually in the same conversations, as generalized personal problems are.

Sometimes, owners have built enough trust with a friend or associate to discuss their concerns in greater detail. This allows the owner to "vent" their fears and concerns in an environment they consider safe. By talking things through in greater depth and detail, with a trusted friend in a confidential setting, there emerges a self-awareness of potential solutions. The very act of frank, open discussion becomes the sounding board for finding seeds of solutions and insights.

However, talking it through out loud, without an honest listener, may produce the effect of an owner answering his own questions and listening to his own answers. Again, subjectivity is involved and their frame of reference hasn't changed at all. The problem may require a differing perspective. The problem may not be solvable by an informal colleague depending on the severity and depth of the issue.

Formal Networks

A more formal network may consist of a regional group that the owner has joined, similar to GPSEG (Greater Philadelphia Senior Executive's Group), BENG (Business Executives Networking Group), MENG (Marketing Executives Networking Group), or FENG (Financial Executives Networking Group). Perhaps there's a group of local owners that meet monthly from a local Chamber of Commerce. These are formal groups that a business owner may belong to and share ideas and networking resources.

> **INSIGHT:**
> *Anyone can give advice but choose only those who listen carefully.*

There are companies that provide more formalized networking support. These include Vistage, YPO, YEO, WEO, TAB and the Chief Executive Network. The formal network provides opportunities for getting to know other owners and for sharing or helping with

INSIGHT

expertise. More progress can be made in these settings where a "forum" of owners attempt to use their skills to help another owner through questioning.

What the owner wants is a safe environment where confidentiality exists and she can source wisdom of business colleagues in whom she can trust.

Generally, when the triggering problem is more threatening, or there is a defined objective such as a sale, succession or acquisition, an owner will seek more formal guidance. At these times informal or even formal networks may not acceptable. It may be a highly confidential situation, or a situation related to the owner's business outlook, financial performance, or even their deepest inner conflicts or fears. In these cases, the owner needs more professional input. And typically that is where a professional Business Advisor can help.

After a short chapter on the science involved in business advice, I will discuss, in depth, the roles of the professional Business Advisor.

❖   ❖   ❖

Chapter 4: The Science of Business Advice

❖   ❖   ❖

The Science of the Brain

To understand more about importance of advice in business, I want to discuss how our brains are built and how they function to understand and internalize advice. By studying what's going on under the hood in our brains, we can better understand people's behaviors and emotions. I promise to provide only enough science to keep things interesting. I believe that neuroscience provides a solid foundation for understanding that the power of advice resides in emotions/heart/ spirit. The personal beliefs and emotions of the business owner are key ingredients for successful change, adaptability, and sustainability.

It May Be All In the Mind

According to research done by Carol S. Dweck, PhD, one of the world's leading researchers in the fields of personality, motivation, social psychology, and developmental psychology, and published in her book: *mindset. The New Psychology of Success*, it is someone's mindset that may hold them back from experiencing the power of advice in business. Dr. Dweck's research shows that *the view someone adopts for themself* profoundly affects the way they lead their life.

Dweck describes two mindsets that determine one's abilities:

- A *fixed mindset* - believing that qualities and capabilities are carved in stone
- A *growth mindset* - the belief that a person's basic qualities are things that can be cultivated through individual efforts

In a fixed mindset, the limiting belief is that someone only has a certain amount of intelligence, a certain personality and a certain moral character and that is the view they adopt and live out. In a growth mindset, everyone can change with growth and experience. The growth mindset involves a belief that a person's true potential is unknown (and unknowable) and that it is impossible to foresee what can be accomplished with years of passion, toil, and training. That means people *can develop* their abilities at most tasks with coaching and practice; that change is possible throughout life. Growth mindsets are possessed by owners who understand that business life is a fascinating process of learning.

Get a Myelin Wrap

Supporting Dweck's mindset theory from a scientific level is Daniel Coyle, author of <u>The Talent Code: Greatness Isn't Born. It's Grown. Here's How</u>. He sums up the science of Dr. Dweck's growth mindset with one word – myelin. Myelin is the insulation that wraps the nerve fibers and plays a key role in the way our brains function, particularly when it comes to acquiring skills. Simply,

Coyle outlines that neurons, our circuit of nerve fibers, is the wiring by which we move, think, and feel. Myelin is the insulation on our neural wiring.

The more myelin that's built up by deep practice and wraps the neural circuitry, the more skilled we become. Myelin builds up over time with practice.

Coyle further states that the story of skill and talent is the story of myelin: *Skill is insulation that wraps neural circuits and grows according to certain signals.*

Coyle describes the process when myelin is "ignited" by a commitment to a deep practice, born out of our deepest unconscious desires. He states that the more an organization embraces the core principles of ignition, deep practice, and master coaching, the more myelin it will build and the more success it will have. In businesses where people are invested in deep practice supported by an owner as a master coach, the rewards of their work is mutual success. As we shall see later, the highly respected college basketball Coach John Wooden was a "myelin driver."

The Meddling Conscious

Another book that helped me to understand decision making is *Incognito: Secret Lives of the Brain* by David Eagleman. I found this book to be of particular importance because the value of any business advice depends on the ability and willingness of the owner to execute it. In this book Eagleman states,

"Almost the entirety of your mental life is not under your conscious control, and the truth is that it's better this way. Consciousness can take the credit it wants, but it is best left at the sidelines for most of the decision making that cranks along in your brain. When it meddles in details it doesn't understand, the operation (of the brain) runs less effectively."

Eagleman's underlying point is that when the brain finds a task it needs to solve, it rewires its own circuitry until it accomplishes the task with maximum efficiency. He calls that process "automatization."

The key point of both books can be illustrated by looking at a task like surfing. On the surface, it looks easy, but it is really quite complex. Surfing requires a great deal of balance, coordination, and visual acuity. However, once it's learned, surfing is something that can be done over and over again at a point where the conscious brain forgets the mechanical details. The physical "how" is now burned into the brain's circuitry. The details are no longer conscious and no longer accessible. This is sometimes called "unconscious competence." You have learned something so well that you no longer need to think about it.

And here's the paradox: once you begin to describe what it is to someone else, it flees conscious description.

The Team of Rivals

Eagleman describes the brains' two main neural systems – the rational and emotional – as a "team-of-rivals" in constant interplay. He points out that:

**In decision making, the emotional system
finalizes the decision in almost all cases.**

Let's build on our surfing metaphor. One surfer described the experience this way:

"When you are waiting for a wave your mind can think a thousand different things. When you paddle for a wave your mind thinks of only a few things. When you catch a wave your mind thinks of only one thing, that one thing is joy. This is why I surf."

"Riding a wave is like a bird riding on the wind. You can feel nature's energy in the waves as you catch it. You cut through the water and glide effortlessly. Sometimes it bends around you so you can ride inside. It's almost a spiritual feeling of being closer to what made us. Then, just as quick as it came, it dies on the shore. You're hooked, and can't wait to go catch another!"

Imagine now that we are on a beach watching a surfer. She's standing, relaxed with her board at her side and watching the ocean swells build waves. She's caught the wave thousands of times. And now she's ready to ride again. She's offered to teach a "grom," a youthful surfer. The guide and the grom paddle out into the swells and turn their boards towards the shore in anticipation of the ride. The grom asks how she will know when to get up? The guide tells her, "Follow me." It's quiet except for the rolling swells against their boards.

The two start paddling hard side-by-side towards shore to catch the top of the next swell that's starting to energize a crest. Both mount their boards. They are perfectly balanced. They feel the rush of the foamy crest and drop into the tube. The force is about to send them into flight. It feels thrilling. A perfect first ride is anticipated by both. Their bodies are receiving a physical response from their unconscious neural network. They are responding to their heightened emotional state. In a lightning strike of consciousness, the grom turns to the guide and asks, *"How do we stay up?"* At that instant the guide and the grom bail off their boards in unison. They are smashed to the sea floor and come up like bobbers, spit out by the next wave. What happened?

Even for people who don't surf, the examples in our everyday lives are many.

Playing a musical instrument, hitting a tennis ball, driving (especially a stick shift), composing text on a computer, even breathing are all physical tasks best done without conscious thought.

That is why serious athletes, artists, writers, and musicians spend so much time on deeply practicing the basics, to automatize them into their unconscious.

> **INSIGHT:**
> *Consciously practice to unconsciously perform.*

Eagleman explains that consciousness is best at setting goals and training the rest of the neural system to meet them. Unfortunately, as we see in the surfer example, consciousness can also interrupt performance by meddling in the neural network. (Did you ever change the right answer to the wrong answer on a standardized test after you had "thought" about it?)

**The quieter their brain is, the better at
something the person becomes.**

As routines get further "automatized," the less conscious access we have to them. Then, if we try to "think" about something that we have learned to do naturally, we lose the unconscious competence and our performance declines.

In our surfing example, the conscious questions made both surfers think about what they were doing, instead of being in the moment and allowing the unconscious circuitry to operate and learn. The practice of automatization gets interrupted and short-circuited by the conscious question posed at the wrong moment by the anxious grom. And so it is with the practice of business.

**We can disrupt learning and performance by
consciously meddling in the practice.**

However, just as these automatized processes, when developed, can enhance performance and success, they can also produce the opposite effect when coupled with fear. We will look further into how fear impacts insight and advice in later chapters.

Mastering Practice

Whatever is practiced based on the owner's outlook on life, the business becomes, much in accordance with the mindset theory of Dr. Dweck. Deep practice in business provides the myelin that wraps the neural circuitry as explored by Coyle. And Eagleman explains the importance of the emotional network to decision making. In sports, one particular coach exemplifies the use of mastering practice in a sports program and that was UCLA basketball Coach John Wooden.

John Wooden was one of the most productive and revered master coaches in college basketball. As was described in his autobiography _Wooden_, Coach Wooden was master at getting individuals to work together for the common good. He showed players how to get the best possible results for the team while at the same time letting each know that they did it themselves.

Wooden describes the power of his personal "sacred trust". He states,

> "A leader, particularly a teacher or coach, has a most powerful influence on those he or she leads, perhaps more than anyone outside the family. Therefore, it is the obligation of the leader, teacher or coach to treat such responsibility as a grave concern. I consider it a sacred trust: helping to mold character, instill productive principles and values, and provide a positive example to those under my supervision. Furthermore, it is a privilege to have that responsibility, opportunity and obligation, one that should never be taken lightly."

Coach Wooden's teaching style consisted of short bursts of focused and intense preparation during practice. These practice directives, while performing repetitive tasks, built his players skills for game time into championship form.

As I look back on my own development as a business owner, I can see that my own mentors influenced me in ways similar to those prescribed by Dweck, Eagleman and Wooden. I first concentrated on developing experiences as an owner, then as a professional manager, and finally as an Advisor to business owners: three very different, yet complimentary, vantage points to study the practice of being in business. With each set of experiences I found out what worked and what didn't work. As Wooden stated, *"Winners make the most mistakes."*

In my years of business practice, I also found that it wasn't necessary for the owner to be the business' best performer.

The work of the owner is leading the people, making decisions, and managing the business.

While each owner needed to be very competent in their work, it was the owner's ability to bring out (or fail to bring out) the individual skills of others that made the difference. It was the ability to build trust, respect, confidence, and loyalty. It was the owner's transition from performer to coach, concentrating on practicing those employee development skills that gave the owner a valuable benefit: freedom.

Personal Creativity

One final point on the science of advice that has made a difference in my advisory practice is honoring the creative process. Mihalyi Csikszentmihalyi, author of *Creativity: Flow and the Psychology of Discovery and Invention,* notes that in order to be creative, one must cultivate curiosity and interest.

I find it is the sense of wonder and awe that inspires me to engage in the creative problem solving and innovation process. Csikszentmihalyi points out that if we learn to enjoy being curious, we cultivate creative flow in our lives. He also states that protecting and conserving that creative energy means disciplining oneself to routinize non-essential tasks in order to allow more time to focus one's energy on what really matters. I heard the statement once that described the value of time:

Guard time with the energy of a tiger.

The real power of the personal creative process is the unconscious. When someone takes the time for reflection and relaxation where no decisions are made, it allows the unconscious to go to work on their behalf. What emerges is generally a conclusion or solution that was previously unforeseen. This is the process of insight. The paradox is the more one consciously tries to solve something, the more the answer eludes them. Sometimes a person just needs to "sleep on it." Unless it's a life-or-death, irreversible matter that's forced upon someone, it's one of the best ways to allow the creative process to work.

What have we learned with the findings and wisdom of Dweck, Coyle, Eagleman, Wooden, and Csikszentmihalyi? One must love their practice, and be diligent in teaching others. The lessons of a growth mindset, deep practice for automatization, the quiet power of the unconscious, the decision making advantage of the emotional neural network, the sacred trust of leadership and cultivating curiosity for creativity are as inspiring as their teachers.

Believe that miracles do happen to those who work hard, and they will appear.

❖　❖　❖

Chapter 5: The Roles of an Advisor

❖ ❖ ❖

The Inspired Generalist

As I outlined in Chapter 1, like medicine, law, and accounting, providing business advice is seen as a professional practice by those of us who take that calling seriously. By a professional practice, I mean that the Advisor must hold him or herself to an exceptionally high standard of honesty, integrity, and commitment to the client who may be basing critical business decisions on that Advisor's research and insights.

Unlike many other professions, a career as an Advisor must be earned. One cannot become a skilled business Advisor by taking an on-line course or even by attending an Ivy League business school. There is no Certification.

Being a Business Advisor is about *who you are* rather than strictly what you know.

Certainly a capable Advisor must know the basics of business: financial statements, business plans, organization charts, and the like. But that knowledge is just the minimum "price of admission."

To be successful and, more importantly, to make the client successful, the Advisor must have passion, insight, integrity, courage, and a number of other critical *personal* characteristics. They must be able to look at the big picture when their client is focused on an immediate crisis. They must dig deep for the underlying truth when those about them a clamoring for a quick fix. They must have the courage to find and speak the truth, and accept the potential costs for doing so. I discuss these characteristics more deeply in Chapter 9.

The Roles of an Advisor

Business advice is something I've applied, studied, researched, and applied some more in my practice. It's a professional practice that, like other professions, can involve different roles under different circumstances.

As I have tried to make abundantly clear in this book, business, particularly business ownership, is a highly personal enterprise. Therefore, the ways in which an Advisor relates to the owner must reflect how that owner experiences their business and the specific needs the owner may have in a particular engagement.

The three basic roles I want to discuss are: Advisor, Consultant, and Coach.

The Advisor Role

First, the Advisor role in and of itself means that I perform research and analysis in order to make recommendations to the business owner or other senior executive. It is up to that owner or executive to make the final decision and arrange for implementation. The Advisor is strictly hands-off. In this role, I am much like one of the various Advisors that the President has for defense, international relations, economics, energy policy, etc. I do the legwork, formulate options and recommendations based on my research, and "speak truth to power."

The Consultant Role

The consultant's role is to provide a level of in-depth expertise and/or operating know-how in a functional business area in a way not currently available inside the organization. Tax consultants, technology consultants, and supply chain consultants are examples. Consultants are typically specialists, not generalists. While they may make recommendations within their functional areas, consultants are usually able to help implement those recommendations. Most businesses do not have expert resources in their ranks to implement a project without help. And as many owners will tell you, the project fails when trying to implement alone.

The Coach Role

A business coach typically works to improve the general skills and business acumen of the client, rather than to address one or more specific issue areas. Therefore, one can find leadership coaches, public speaking coaches, "dress for success" coaches, and even general business coaches.

Additionally, cultural development and assembling the right team members with the right strengths is a valuable coaching role.

There are many books and assessments available for understanding individual strengths. What comes to mind is the Kolbe Indexes for natural abilities and instinctual strengths by Kathy Kolbe (www.kolbe.com) and the Gallup StrengthsFinder (www.strengthsfinder.com) based on work by Marcus Buckingham & Donald O. Clifton, Ph.D. Coaching a non-performing team to high performance is something I have done in several executive assignments as a professional manager. An external Advisor as coach has similar capabilities to influence the team members, but without the authority to hire and fire.

A given professional may assume any or all of these roles, depending on the client needs and the nature of the engagement or they might restrict their practice to a niche and simply turn down other opportunities. Additionally, these role definitions may seem confusing because practitioners often

> **INSIGHT:**
> *Asking for help is powerful; suffering in silence is pitiful.*

use them interchangeably. Salespeople often call themselves consultants, consultants can call themselves coaches, accountants often call themselves advisors. The names are not that important, but the role that they play in a company is. Owners need to be clear about what they expect from an outside expert or downstream problems will emerge.

For the purposes of this book, I will focus on the specific role of Business Advisor as a generalist with financial expertise. That is my "sweet spot" and my practice.

It is the area where I have learned the most and about which I have the most to say.

In my view, the Business Advisor is someone who looks holistically at the big picture surrounding a specific business issue. Advisors dig up, identify, and assimilate relevant facts and insights and apply them to the current situation in order to offer insight and direction.

Additionally, I view the ability of an Advisor to be especially skilled in one or more key disciplines of business, be they strategic, financial, or operational as an underlying asset. An Advisor need not be an expert in a niche discipline, but, to be effective, they must deeply understand the practice of business.

In addition, in any given advisory engagement, I see the Advisor also acting in the capacity of a business coach, working closely with the client to mentor and teach. In this manner, Advisors provide a source of sustainability as clients eventually learn how the Advisor works and develop those skills for themselves.

In this chapter we will look at the basis for advising, the sources owners use for advice, and why some owners may resist formal advice. I will discuss what triggers the need for advice and describe transition points in business. And I'll outline the value of advice, including the strengths and weaknesses of internal and external advice. Then I will make the best case I can for engagement with an Advisor.

Professional Advice

There are literally tens of thousands of people and organizations out there that claim to provide business advice. However, despite the fact that many of them promote themselves as business Advisors, they are not all alike nor do they all perform the same services in the same way.

I can categorize these business professionals as follows:

- **Professional Support**
  Support professionals include attorneys, CPA's, recruiters, etc. These individuals and organizations are essential to any business because of their expertise in areas where businesses can get into legal trouble. These professionals can be a great source of advice in their areas of expertise and some of them also have skills as general business Advisors.

  However it is a rare combination of experience for an accounting or legal professional to have actual, hands-on experience owning or operating a variety of businesses. So temper your expectations as to how deeply these professionals may go towards helping you solve business operating issues or providing potential options to do so.

- **Coaches & Consultants**
  These were discussed at the beginning of this chapter

- **Training Organizations**
  There are a number of organizations that provide business training and post-training consulting and advice. The best known include Dale Carnegie, Sandler Systems, and the American Management Association.

- **Consulting Firms**
  Consulting firms can vary from the huge (Accenture, Deloitte and McKinsey) to one or two-person shops. As discussed at the beginning of the chapter, consultants tend to focus on particular subject matter expertise. The larger firms usually

have departments that specialize, even if the firm presents itself as general.

One danger with the larger firms is that they tend to have institutionalized processes and procedures they follow when addressing certain business problems. While effective in the long run for larger companies, these procedures can be very expensive for smaller firms, and may sometimes even be inappropriate or excessive.

- **Academics**

  Many business school professors do consulting on the side. These professionals can be a great source for businesses because good professors strive to keep up with the latest thinking in their field. On the other hand, academics may have less first hand business experience than other types of Advisors or, in many cases, none at all.

- **Group Consulting**

  Some organizations, such as Vistage or TAB put business owners together in a forum or group to discuss their issues with each other with the assistance of a moderator called a "Chair" who is a franchise holder. These groups typically consist of 10-15 non-competitive executives who meet once or twice per month. The Chair may also provide other consulting services outside the group.

- **Free Advisory Services**

  There are governmental and non-profit organizations that provide business advice, usually on a local level. These include SBDCs (Small Business Development Centers),

SCORE (Service Corps of Retired Executives), and Chambers of Commerce.

- **Professional Business Advisors**
  These individuals, including me and my firm, focus on assisting business owners and executives in a one-to-one setting to make the best decisions they can regarding any number of business transition matters.

Internal & External Advisors

Owners can obtain good advice from both internal and external sources. I need to be careful here to point out that identifying sources for excellent advice is not an either/or proposition. As an owner, you should be getting all the good advice you can from all the knowledgeable sources that you trust. While I encourage business owners to retain a professional Advisor who focuses on their specific needs and goals, there are many other places owners can get advice, both generally and regarding specific issues.

So let's say an owner has a substantial and successful business. That owner might look around at their executive team and wonder:

- What advice can I routinely rely upon from my key people?
- Which one of them can cross over several disciplines when needed?
- Which ones are teachers and could be mentors?
- Who really thinks through what's going on here and can reflect on the impacts of potential decisions?

- Who can size up a situation and provide me multiple options?

If the owner has made the process of giving and getting advice a part of their organizational culture, I believe that they are likely to feel pretty good about the answers they receive. On the other hand, if the owner is not feeling so sure about the team, it may be because advisory qualities may not be evident in that team.

There are strengths and weaknesses in both internal and external advisors. When internal advisors are used properly, owners may have much more in the way of advisory resources than they thought they did.

Internal Advisors

Internal advisors are the best sources for information about what is really going on inside and immediately outside of the business. Those internal advisors may occupy various roles within your business. For example, sales people (not necessarily your VP of Sales or Sales Manager, unless they are out in the field) are usually an excellent source for information about customers, competitors, and product benefits and problems. Administrative assistants and receptionists will know far more about internal organizational politics than anyone else.

The big problem with internal advisors is that it may be difficult to assess the objectivity of their information and advice.

Many Presidents/CEO of privately-held organizations have identified key people upon whom they can rely for frank, open, and honest input. It may be the Executive Assistant or the CFO or a long-term sales person who has "been through the wars" with the owner. Here are some of the pluses and minuses of having an internal advisor:

Strengths of an Internal Advisor

An effective internal advisor:

- Knows the owners' temperament.
- Has built trust with the owner over a long time.
- Is personally loyal towards the owner.
- Understands company history as a context for making any recommendation.
- Knows about the industry and company environment.
- Usually willing to provide advice as part of their regular job and may feel honored to be asked.
- Is readily accessible.

Weaknesses of an Internal Advisor

However, sometimes an internal advisor:

- May hold back for fear of repercussions if wrong or controversial.
- May feel it's not their place to tell the boss what to do.
- Because they work for the same organization, may share some of the owner's biases.
- May be biased against initiatives that might negatively impact their job or position in the company.
- May expect special treatment because of close relationship with owner.

- Should insider leave, there may be confidentiality risks.

This list highlights the trade-offs for using internal advisors. On the other hand, it is impossible not to get internal input and advice unless the owner wants to operate in a complete vacuum.

Therefore, when gathering input and advice from those inside the company, owners need to ask:

- How could this issue or decision impact the person offering the advice?
- Is that person in a position to have objective information?
- In what other ways might this person be biased?
- Can I trust that person to keep what we say confidential?
- What would be the potential negative impact if confidentiality were broken?

It is important to realize that everybody, both inside and outside your organization has biases. The key is trying to understand what the biases might be and the underlying reward/consequence system that may have created them.

External Advisors

External Advisors are required in three primary circumstances.

- When a fresh, totally objective perspective is needed.
- When specific expertise or credentials are needed.
- When the decision will have such an impact on employees or customers that strict confidentiality is mandatory.

The External Advisor brings objectivity, observations, critical thinking, calculated risks, deep business knowledge, and a multiplicity of subject matter understanding to the owner's problem. In addition, they usually bring their own network of other potential resources.

Over a long period of time in the same organization, an Advisor may eventually lose the level of objectivity and neutrality they had when they were first engaged. The owner must realize this when it happens but still may elect to remain engaged relying on the Advisor's contribution as a long-term member of an Advisory Board.

In the chapter on Guiding Virtues, I will explore characteristics seen in the most effective Advisors. For purposes of comparison to the points and tradeoffs of engaging an Internal Advisor, I have outlined below a similar matrix of strengths and weaknesses of the External Advisor:

Strengths of an External Advisor

An effective external advisor:

- Is collaborative in style.
- Maintains a respectfully honest approach in determining what the owner wants.
- Is a clean slate for building a trust relationship.
- Has loyalty that is driven by personal respect for the owner and the company and by a professional respect for integrity and objectivity.
- Can get valuable 360 input from key team members to utilize as a context for making a recommendation.

- From an outsider perspective, has broad base of experiences that can inform decision making and is free of the biases of industry-specific knowledge.
- Maintains a deep and broad network to tap for solving complex problems.
- Has a beginning and an end of service as defined by the scope of work or engagement letter.

There is a unique role for confusion which is both strength and a weakness. By introducing new concepts the External Advisor unbalances the *status quo*. This leads to newer and fresher thinking but also leads to resistance and misunderstanding due to new sets of assumptions and processes not yet in place.

Weaknesses of an External Advisor

However, sometimes an external advisor:

- May not be as sensitive to the owner's temperament as they might like.
- Trust may be low in early engagement and built over time and performance results.
- Until trust in the outsider is developed, key team members may clam up or mislead.
- Unless there are aspects that drive quantifiable results and sustainability there's risk of results not being clearly attributable to the investment in the Advisor.
- May have less industry-specific knowledge.

Having looked at the strengths and weakness of internal and external advisors, let's move on to understanding the case for engagement of an Advisor and how an owner might find an Advisor worth engaging.

The Case for Engagement

Many times, and in many circumstances, I've heard the following from clients, *"I'm just amazed. If I had to find someone like you, I don't know where I would go out and look."* Or others have told me, *"I didn't know a service even existed like this. We are so lucky we found you when we did."* And it's all true.

One of the issues that we face as business Advisors is getting the word out about the services we perform. Like many other business owners, we must manage and market our practice as well as do the work. Sometimes it's a demanding ride, but clients come first.

Frequently, we do our work quietly and without fanfare. Due to the confidentiality involved, we know we cannot promote our work specifically at a company.

We usually cannot even disclose the names of many of our clients.

I market my services by building trusted referral networks among professionals such as attorneys, accountants, bankers, non-traditional lenders, financial planners, wealth managers, and trust officers. Referrals from these support professionals may be the only way an owner or family member would know that someone like me exists. Sometimes owners find Advisors at trade associations, Chambers of Commerce, or networks of like-minded business owners in non-competitive businesses.

As I've discussed, the right External Business Advisor may be difficult to find. Quite typically, they are on engagement and in demand. However, the best time to contact a potential Advisor is when they are not needed immediately.

A forward-thinking owner will take the time to get to know the Business Advisors who practice in the community in order to see if they feel comfortable with them.

Having the contact and connection may one day serve quite well, especially if advisory assistance is needed in an emergency.

Opening the Door to Possibilities

Many times, the demands of operating a business do not allow an owner the time to step back and see the business from other vantage points or to develop expertise in specialized business areas. An Advisor can tap their experiences with a diverse group of business to find new possibilities that never would have occurred to an owner focused on the daily management of their business.

> **INSIGHT:**
> *Common sense is not so common.*

In other words, it is the Advisor's job to remain "outside the box" and unconstrained by the "conventional wisdom" in any specific industry.

With this in mind, it is important that owners not surrender to the temptation to retain Advisors that are too much like them personally or who have spent their careers in the owner's industry. While retaining an Advisor the owner can easily relate to personally and professionally may initially seem like a good idea, objective perspective requires differences. At the same time, the Advisor cannot be *too* different or it will be difficult to establish trust. I recommend that owners try to strike a balance.

Advisor as Generalist

An Advisor may serve an owner in a variety of circumstances. I have led engagements dealing with such diverse issues as:

- Sourcing New Lines of Business
- Preparation for an Acquisition
- Exit Planning & Preparation
- Valuation Assessment
- Technology Recovery
- Mentoring Key Executives
- Post-Sale Integration
- Preparing a Succession Plan
- Organizing an Estate
- Turnaround Management
- Acting Executive Management
- Identifying Professionals
- Strategic Sales Development
- Forecasting & Prediction
- Disability or Illness
- Lead Negotiator
- Debt Re-Structuring
- Change Management
- Growth Planning
- Networking

Where I have not had sufficient personal expertise in a certain area, I tapped into my extensive network of professionals to provide it. I continued to coordinate the entire project in support of the owner's objectives.

As a facilitator, an Advisor can nurture discussions that are sensitive between parties in conflict. It may be the mediation of views or beliefs, whereby a third party facilitator may more easily talk through the "elephant in the room" that everyone is ignoring. The Advisor may become a confidante with whom fears of the owner are entrusted, allowing the owner to unburden themselves.

Listening with understanding is extremely helpful to an owner, as is the feedback of content or fears that are being confronted.

This allows the owner to process feedback, without immediate judgment, and can be very effective for the owner in arriving at new solutions.

Advice in Business

I have discussed the three roles of giving and getting advice in business – as an advisor, consultant, and business coach, consolidated into the one role I consider the highest for business advice – Business Advisor. I've reviewed transition points that occur in business, and why owners seek advice and why they may resist advice. I've also outlined the benefits of advice and the strengths and weaknesses of the internal & external advisor. In closing, I've made the case for engaging an Advisor and have bulleted circumstances in business that may initiate use of an Advisor.

My overall efforts in this chapter were to provide an overview of the various roles of an Advisor and the various strengths and weaknesses of an Internal and External Advisor.

❖   ❖   ❖

Chapter 6: When Business Advice Matters Most

❖   ❖   ❖

The Business Ownership Lifecycle

There are three distinct stages to any entrepreneurial venture:

1. Starting A Business
2. Staying In Business
3. Transitioning A Business

Starting a Business

When people think of entrepreneurship, the first thing that usually comes to mind is the process of starting a business: the "big idea," the business plan, funding, etc. There are a large number of excellent books, blogs, and courses on how to do this. There are also plenty of consultants, business development programs and angel investors interested in assisting new businesses to get started. There are government programs at the Federal, state, and local levels, as well as "incubators" at many large universities. Although starting a business requires advice (and I have started up five different businesses), it is not the stage I want to focus on for this book. Rather, the stages of business where I have seen the extraordinary occur are in the staying in business and transitioning a business and where an Advisor's insight matters most.

Staying in Business

Staying in business is much harder than starting a business. No matter what someone may know about business, about their particular work, or about people, there will be continual surprises and problems that are outside of that person's current levels of knowledge and experience. This is where outside advice can be extremely valuable.

Paradoxically, this is also where businesses are least likely to retain a professional Advisor. As long as things seem to be going alright, business owners are reluctant to incur the cost of a professional Advisor. Usually, it is not until there is a crisis that the owner seeks help. Then it may be too late. A colleague once said,

"It's less costly to prevent a problem than it is to fix a problem."

Transitioning a Business

This is the really hard part in business because there's a build-up of emotional investment after many years of sweat. In my experience, only a small percentage of business owners plan for their exit from the business.

Even after a lifetime of hard work, sacrifice, and investment, very few owners prepare for their biggest payday.

Business schools and entrepreneurial programs seldom discuss the complexities, the costs, or the legalities of an exit. This is a major body of knowledge which impacts business value, and what is eventually left for the owner to invest or spend once the business sale is consummated.

There are, however, plenty of business attorneys, business brokers, and consultants standing ready to help the moment an owner has decided to exit. Again, this unprepared attempt to exit the business tends to happen as a last resort after problems have arisen and the value of the business has declined. It's really not ideal because the owner may be forced to think in terms of scarcity rather than abundance. And taking the business to market under these conditions usually does not yield the highest price.

I recommend that owners engage a Business Advisor as soon as they start *considering* their exit strategy. That Advisor should:

- Be skilled in the marketing, packaging and selling of businesses.
- Understand how to add value to the selling process.
- Be experienced at leading negotiations.
- Know how to solicit, identify, and qualify Buyers who can actually pull the trigger on the sale.
- There's evidence that engaging a professional Business Advisor in this area yields at least a 20% higher enterprise value for the business owner. Selling the business is only one transition.

Planning the Exit

Habit 2 of Steven Covey's famous book _The Seven Habits of Highly Effective People_ is "Begin with the end in mind." From that perspective, I recommend to business owners that they should decide on their transition goals early, because this decision will impact decision making over the entire life of the company.

If there are partners or investors involved, making this exit strategy explicit can be critical. Some of the most difficult advisory engagements I have had involved partners who had conflicting expectations about how and when they were going to exit the company. It is best when everyone agrees and there are few surprises later when one party wants to leave or sell, but the other does not.

A business owner has three basic strategies for exiting the business. These are:

- Sell the company to new owners.
- Keep the company and pass ownership eventually to heirs.
- Dissolve the company.

Each has certain pros and cons and each requires careful planning to make that transition successful. Even if the owner has not decided what to do, it is still vital to do the planning. In fact,

I recommend that business owners prepare for all three possibilities – sale, succession and dissolution.

As discussed above, circumstances may take the choice out of their hands, and prior preparation will help maintain asset value in any of these circumstances.

Selling the Company

Selling their company usually requires some significant rethinking for most business owners. Their company is their "baby." Significant parts of their self-esteem are tied up in how successful the company has been and what kind of reputation it has. In other words, the company usually has great intrinsic as well as extrinsic value to its owner.

Unless the company is being sold to a relative or an insider who has been intimately involved during much of the company's development, an outside purchaser will not care how much the owner loves it. Potential purchasers will look at the company through their own lens, not the owner's. The key thing to remember is that:

**Any company is only worth what someone else
is willing to pay for it!**

From this perspective, think of a company as a product. Begin to develop a marketing plan for the company. What would be of value to others? What types of buyers would be interested? Remember that some buyers might want to keep running the firm as it is, while others might just be interested in key assets (e.g., technology, customer base, physical plant).

**The process of selling a company can be complex and frustrating.
It is always emotional for the owner and
often for the employees.**

There are numerous books on the subject and eventually, I may write my own.

At this point, however, I have three important suggestions:

- Continue to focus on building value.
- Keep meticulous records; they may be required one day.
- Employ professionals to advise in the process.

Keeping the Company

I think most business owners would like to see their creations endure. It still makes me smile to see my first business still operating. It's nice to know that your retirement is provided for and that your family will have a source of passive income for years to come. This goal seems easy, but is often difficult to attain without extensive planning.

The first step is to develop succession plans for both the management and the ownership of the business. If the business is to endure, it must remain in the hands of people who will take care of it and are competent to do so.

The second step is estate planning. Many of our most difficult business advisory engagements involved feuds among heirs. Had I not been involved, much of the estate would have been wasted fighting the legal battles and the company would have been irreparably damaged. Also, no buyer wants to acquire a company when there is even a hint of litigation.

Dissolving the Company

Many business owners are under the mistaken impression that all one has to do is lock the doors and walk away. Nothing could be further from the truth. Most businesses have legal responsibilities to employees, customers & clients, suppliers, regulatory agencies, and taxing entities. Many of these responsibilities do not disappear, just because the company is no longer in business. In particular, tax liabilities and compliance matters may not even go away in bankruptcy.

If the plan is to simply close the business one day, it is critical to ensure that legal liabilities are minimized and that contracts cover the owner in case of liabilities.

Value Creation

Today more than ever before, the emphasis in financial management is on growing cash flow and building value.

Just ask any banker about the importance of debt service coverage ratios! Every stakeholder with a financial interest is wondering about mitigating risks and improving cash flow. We are also at a socio-demographic point where there will be fewer and fewer qualified buyers in the future. That means only the best businesses will eventually be sold and the current owner's sweat equity may or may not count for much in the marketplace.

That's why the single most important financial metric in evaluating the progress of a privately held business is fair market value.

By identifying those activities that build and drive value, the owner will get a much better return when it's time to exit the business.

Crisis Response

Crises in business are inevitable. You may even be in one right now! When in crisis, the pressure is intense. Owners become hyper-focused on short-term management and may have a hard time identifying creative solutions to the problem itself. Many times an owner might wonder who they could turn to for business insight and assistance. That's where a Business Advisor may be invaluable.

Advisors can assist in identifying new options, prioritizing short term activities, and implementing effective crisis management strategies. Depending upon their qualifications, they can also help renegotiate financial arrangements, if required. By receiving steady decision support the owner may preserve assets and maintain cash flow until the clouds disappear.

> **INSIGHT:**
> *The more you focus on fixing, the more broken things you'll find.*

It's not that an Advisor has all the answers, it's more that asking the right questions makes the difference in driving the right decisions.

That's where an Advisor is an invaluable ally to the owner.

Getting Unstuck

From time to time owners may feel like the organization is spinning its wheels. There's a method to creating momentum and making progress and if applied wisely, it can yield significant value. Many times routines and old habits reign, people remain unchallenged and business progress stagnates. The business the owner dreamed of becomes a "golden noose" rather than a golden goose. People and systems can become "stuck" over time and the owner can become more tired. That's when it may be time to plan and make a healthy change.

An Advisor knows that executing a vision takes methodical preparation. Knowing and predicting next steps takes a valid assessment and a keen sense of timing along with an understanding of human behavior and motivation.

**Being prepared to execute a change provides
confidence during times of transformation.**

An Advisor may be the outside influence that's needed to help the owner get traction driving towards new goals for the organization.

Planning for Contingencies

In his bestselling book, _The Black Swan_, Nassim Taleb argues that most of the events in history that have had the greatest impact on humanity have been those rare, unpredictable events he calls Black Swans. Examples include the 9-11 attacks, the internet and housing bubbles, political assassinations, etc. We have all experienced times when our lives were radically altered, sometimes for the better, sometimes for the worse, by an unforeseen event or a random choice.

These Black Swans are a fact of life for business owners. Unfortunately, most business owners are so focused on managing the everyday that they fail to notice the potential opportunities and threats that surround them. They do not have any contingency plans in place and, as a result, an unforeseen opportunity or problem can quickly become a crisis.

Here are some examples:

Lost Opportunities

- **Breakthrough product/service**
  You may identify a potentially profitable opportunity for your firm, but not have the resources available to pursue it because all of your funds are already committed.

- **Blue Birds**
  A potential customer suddenly approaches you with a large order that you cannot accept because you had downsized to save costs and increase short term profits.

Negative Events

- **Illness or death**
  Few things throw a privately help business into as much chaos as the sudden illness or death of the owner.

- **Loss of key person**
  Similar to the loss of an owner, the loss of a key employee (sales manager, head of R&D) can create serious problems.

- **Sudden change in business conditions**
  We have all experienced one or more these types of events: the loss of a key customer, an imposed change in financing arrangements, a strong competitive attack, a law suit, etc.

Part of the practice of business ownership is to "expect unexpected events." For example:

- **It is never too early to put a succession plan in place.** Hopefully, it will never be used in an emergency. However, the process of hiring, training, and evaluating potential successors can be very valuable in and of itself. The process not only provides reassurance that the company will continue to be well managed if something happens to you, it also encourages you to think about exactly what you do and how you do it.

- **As suggested above, having a contingency fund is critical.** Without one, an owner will not be able to respond aggressively to either opportunities or threats.

Setting a Vision

Most companies fail to grow not because product or management issues, but rather because they continue to do what they have always been successful at and fail to appreciate the new opportunities that the marketplace may be presenting.

An Advisor with diverse operating experience can provide a deep appreciation for the rapid evolution of today's business environment. In fact, cross-industry experience enables a skilled Advisor to identify and evaluate previously unrecognized growth opportunities and develop effective marketing strategies for capitalizing on them.

By working closely with the owner, an Advisor may be able to offer new and profitable perspectives for products, services or lines of business. There may also be niche' markets, international demand and potential supply chain consolidations that are available. This is where an owner's vision can be shaped into an action plan prepared carefully and aligned with calculated risk.

There may also be time considerations that impact the owner's vision. Organic growth may mean slugging it out in the marketplace, which can be much slower. Diversifying or acquiring the strategic potential may be more advantageous in the long run even though it may be a larger risk of capital investment.

These and other considerations for implementing the owner's vision require preparation and a written executable plan, which the Advisor may help quantify, identify, qualify and define. Transforming owner vision to an operating reality with increased value is where an Advisor may provide multiples of return.

Diversifying the Company

Diversification of the business is a way for the owner to offset risk. It's no different with professionally managed financial portfolios. Over concentration on specific customers, product lines, or services can be devastating when major change takes place, especially if it is sudden and out of the owner's control. However, diversification also inherently carries with it a level of risk and needs close evaluation and analysis.

By performing an internal assessment, there may be potential for diversifying within the existing client base. Or there may be justification for diversifying product lines or services based on market demand. An owner may want to be on the lookout for these potential opportunities and, before investing time, energy, and capital, evaluate potential opportunities with the help of an Advisor. There have been many businesses that started with one product line and then successfully diversified into multiple product lines to allay the fears of investors.

Perhaps the insight that can be gained before investing is worth the potential disappointment of a failed experiment that has the potential to chip away at or capsize the core business.

Acquiring a Company

The acquisition of a target company may make sense for strategic growth. Acquisitions also may yield valuable personnel, technologies, an existing customer base, and operating economies of scale.

Acquisitions also may bring unforeseen risks as assets may not end up being as claimed and cultural differences may override operating economies.

To that end, investing in an Advisor to work closely on an acquisition makes sense.

It also may take heavy financial analysis to uncover potential risks and rewards. That's where an Advisor may be an ideal asset to the owner in working through "what if" scenarios. Skilled at listening, asking the right questions, financial analysis, option models, forecasting, data research, and market research, an Advisor offers the owner an independent view. The key value in strategic acquisition is to be able to integrate the opportunity and mitigate its risks.

By having an Advisor perform the analysis, the owner is likely to get an objective and frank perspective. Internal bias may miss certain deal points or value points altogether. And when it comes to negotiating an acquisition, the owner may be well served by an external, independent Advisor who can assist in evaluating offers, responses, and agreements.

Acquisitions take time and may take on a life of their own. If not led by a seasoned negotiator and transaction-savvy professional who knows the potential pitfalls on the path, the acquisition process can be filled with complexity.

Additionally, an owner may lose sight of the initial reason for the acquisition and become too obsessed with the kill in the hunt and may lose perspective. For these reasons, an Advisor may serve the owner as a skilled intermediary who can advance the acquisition process methodically, vet the potential targets efficiently, and provide the owner with an objective, emotional buffer.

Setting Goals

"Be careful what you wish for, you just might get it."

Goals are critical to any business success. But they have to be the right goals. I have seen many businesses fail even when they were meeting the goals that owners had set for them. I have also seen businesses that appeared to be failing when, in fact, the owners were looking at the wrong success criteria.

For most business owners, personal goals and business goals are interlinked. As stated earlier, people own businesses for very personal reasons. Some of those reasons may even be contradictory. Without clear, measurable goals for both near and long terms, owners can easily be confused about what they most need to be doing.

However, setting clear goals can:

- Focus thinking
- Help define action
- Identify needed resources
- Cut waste
- Measure success

At the same time, if goals are too tightly defined or too restrictive, owners may miss seeing even better opportunities that may present themselves later.

The Five Step Goal Setting Process

Bob uses a five step process to help define powerful and appropriate goals for business. (This material comes from his book *The Entrepreneur's Guide to Marketing* and is used with his explicit permission.) This process allows a business owner (or anyone else) to analyze each goal for relevance and clarity.

1. What do I want?

This is the initial statement of a goal as we usually think about it. For example:

- I want a $100,000/year income.
- I want my children to have a good education.
- I want to increase my profits.
- I want to grow by 15% per year.
- I want to be the premier company in my industry.

Because business is personal, business owners and Advisors need to think about goals very carefully, and clarify in their own minds whether each goal is primarily business or personal and whether the goals conflict in any way.

2. How will I know I have it?

This step defines the criteria by which success in achieving the goal will be evaluated.

A goal is of no use if the owner cannot tell whether or not they have reached it. For example, if the goal is "To be the premier provider of widgets to the technology business community in the Eastern United States," how would the owner ever know they had succeeded? What does "premier" mean? Who decides? Which businesses are and are not part of the "technology business community?" Should the business ignore Ohio in order to focus on New Jersey? Should the business ignore other potentially profitable products and manufacture only widgets? An experienced Advisor can be extremely valuable in clarifying both success criteria and strategic alternatives.

Chances are that the owner has some idea, maybe just an unconscious idea, as to what they have in mind when they set a goal. When success criteria are articulated, motivation and direction toward achieving that goal are greatly improved. And the more detailed and specific the owner and Advisor are with defining success criteria, the more motivated the owner and everyone else in the organization will feel.

As an example, I commonly hear business owners say that they want to increase their profits. But what do they *really* want?

First of all, what do they mean by profit? Is it:

> **INSIGHT:**
> *Expect nothing and you may get it, so visualize the goal.*

- Gross margin?
- Operating profit?
- Taxable profit?
- Positive cash flow?
- Net profit after taxes and depreciation?
- Measured in percentage?
- Measured in total dollars?

These can yield very different, even contradictory numbers. Or, by "increasing profit" are they planning to:

- Raise prices?
- Increase sales?
- Cut costs?
- Eliminate certain less profitable products/services?

Each of these strategies can lead to increased profits. Again, the choice here is critical.

And once the success parameters are chosen, the owner must then decide how much things need to change and by when. A well-formed profit goal would then look like:

> **"Our goal is to increase net dollar profit by**
> **18% over the next twelve months."**

Now the owner has a goal that has a clear deadline and a clear method to measure its achievement.

3.   What will it mean to me to have it?

This step looks at the importance of a goal, the value that is placed on it. Is this goal critical to financial survival, self-esteem, or some other aspect of personal/family health or welfare? In other words, is the goal essential to the business or the owner or is it simply something desirable?

What usually happens is that when people start looking closely at what a particular goal means to them, they become aware that their goal is really tied to some other, deeper, more emotional goal. I may want a Mercedes because I want to impress my neighbors or clients, or because my father drove one, or because one of my children was injured in a car accident and I think Mercedes are extremely safe. Goals may even (often) be nested three or four levels deep and/or may relate to several deeper needs.

For example: I want the $300,000 income so I can save a lot of money and so I can buy all the things I want my children to have. I want to save money so that my family will be secure. I want to save money so that I feel secure if something happens to me. I want my children to have all the good things I never had (or did have). You get the point.

Now go back to the business example from before. Why would the owner want to increase profits? This question is more important than it seems. It is the underlying motivation toward this goal that will be the greatest determinant of success. For example, is the underlying motivation:

- More personal income?
- Investment in growth?
- New product development?
- Environmental change?
- Competitive pressure?

Again, each of these may suggest a different level of need and a different approach to goal achievement. An important part of the Advisor's job is to help the owner get clear here.

In addition, each of these may suggest a new set of goals. For example, if I am interested in increasing profits because I really want to get additional money to finance new product development, I have to ask myself why I want the new product. If it is to create more profit, am I in a chicken and egg situation?

In my experience, most businesses have these unexamined, un-clarified goals. Fortunately, these goals will get resolved when they are examined carefully.

4.   What will get in my way?
This is where it starts to get practical. Examining the practicality of our wants and goals is something that many people do not do, and, in fact, may avoid doing.

Practicality can be looked at from two vantage points. The first is internal: How will my own attitudes and behavior get in the way? The second is external: What external circumstances could prevent me from getting what I want? It is important that both be examined. Sometimes we are inclined to blame the outside world for things which we are responsible for ourselves and sometimes we blame ourselves for things we have no control over. If we are unwilling to be ruthlessly honest with ourselves and with our environment, we have set up barriers to the achievement of our goal.

There are always both internal and external hurdles to accomplishing any goal. The key is in recognizing what we can and cannot control. Even if we have an accurate view of the external obstacles that we face in reaching our goal, we can still sabotage ourselves by:

- Stressing out over things we cannot control.
- Avoiding (consciously or unconsciously) taking responsibility for things that we can, in fact, control.

This concept is best summarized by the famous Serenity Prayer:

"God, Grant me the Serenity to accept the things I cannot change,
The Courage to change the things I can,
And the Wisdom to know the difference."

Most people have mixed feelings about almost everything they want. Goals may appear to conflict or require trade-offs: e.g., the owner may want to provide the best of everything for their family and, at the same time, want to save money for retirement. An owner may think that a particular goal is impossible, e.g., too much competition, poor economy, etc. or may feel inadequate, unworthy, overwhelmed, or hold any number of other negative beliefs that get in the way of reaching that goal. An owner may be prone to procrastination, over-commitment, or any of a number of other behaviors which inhibit their ability to reach the goal.

It is important to recognize that goals do not exist "in a vacuum." There will always be ideas, beliefs, and other important goals which may conflict with, inhibit, or otherwise interfere with what an owner may want to do. Becoming successful in the long term involves a willingness to face up to all of these issues. Advisors can help.

At the same time, there are likely to be barriers over which we have no control.

Many "motivational" speakers and self-help books will try to convince people that there is nothing that cannot accomplished if they so choose. And that may be true if there is only one goal and someone spends all of their energy on achieving it.

Most of us lead more complicated lives and experience many dreams and have many responsibilities that we choose not to abandon in search of some single Holy Grail. For me, it is important to clearly assess the constraints that life has placed on me (or that I have chosen to place on myself) in order to assess the actual time, energy, emotional effort, money, etc. that I would have to invest in achieving any one goal.

Let's return to the business example. What would be some of the constraints to increasing profits? It obviously depends on the strategy used. Suppose the strategy is cutting costs while maintaining competitive pricing. Any of the following could get in the way of this strategy being successful:

- Increased competitive price pressure
- Long term contracts with important customers
- Labor contracts
- Increasing energy prices or other uncontrollable external forces
- Loyalty to workers
- Commitment to a particular location
- Reluctance to outsource off-shore

5. What will I commit to in order to get it?

This is, of course, the investment question. This is the point at which the owner and Advisor must look at what really has to be done in order to achieve the goal. How much time will it take? How much money? What other goals must be set aside? Who else might be impacted? In other words, what are the trade-offs?

As the owner honestly examines what that will take to achieve a particular goal, it may turn out that they have underestimated the investment necessary, or over-estimated the benefit to be received. In either case, they may want to re-examine that goal. Or, as is sometimes the case, they may have overestimated what it will take and thereby begin to experience the goal as much more possible. Now motivation will increase, pleasure in approaching the task will increase, and the likelihood of achieving the goal will greatly increase.

Goal Conflicts

Bob's father once said,

"You can have anything, but you can't have everything."

Goal conflicts are a fact of life for business owners. There are constant demands for scarce resources of time and capital. There is the desire to reward employee loyalty by promoting from within against the need to bring in fresh ideas by hiring outsiders. There is the reluctance to introduce new products that might cannibalize the sales of established products. The list goes on.

My experience has shown that goal conflicts generally fall into one or more the following four categories:

1. **Personal rewards vs. business investment**
   Given all the hard work that the owner typically puts in and the high degree of risk that the owner assumes, it is only natural for the owner to expect a lion's share of the rewards.

   An important part of the practice of ownership is maintaining the balance between personal/family needs and the needs of the business.

2. **Loyalty to people vs. loyalty to the business**
   As a business grows and evolves, its personnel and partner needs also grow and evolve. Employees, suppliers, bankers, attorneys, and others who may have been invaluable at the early stages of the business may become obsolete as the business grows. Sticking with people who can no longer provide the expertise the business needs does not serve either party in the long run. Similarly, "dumping" people as soon as they cease to be useful is also a bad strategy. The most valuable employees quickly learn that everyone in the firm is disposable and seek employment elsewhere.

**The best strategy is to continually train valuable
employees to keep up with the needs of the
business and be honest with people who
will eventually be let go.**

Give them as much time as possible to find a new job even
if it means losing them earlier than would be preferred. The
company's reputation for loyalty will make it easier and less
expensive to hire and keep the great people later.

3. **External demands vs. internal needs**
   Privately-held businesses are under constant pressure from
   bankers, suppliers, employees, and, sometimes, family
   members to meet certain performance goals or implement
   certain strategies.

**While it is essential that external stakeholders be
kept happy, that should not be done at the
expense of making decisions that hurt
the firm in the long run.**

4. **Long term vs. short term**
   - Long Term Goals – What I want most
   - Short Term Goals – What I want now
   The habit of sacrificing what is wanted most for what is wanted
   now is one of the major causes of entrepreneurial failure.

**Some have referred to a constant focus on the short
term as "The discount rate on future disaster."**

In fact, there is research that shows that the willingness to
defer short term gratification for long term benefits is one of

the best discriminators between successful and unsuccessful people, in general.

The key to dealing with goal conflicts is balance. Learning to balance between the changing and conflicting goals of an organization is critical to the practice of ownership.

Impacting the Ownership Lifecycle

There are two major ways to impact the Business Ownership Lifecycle: planning for change and preparing for transition. These are simple but powerful recipes for positive transformations.

Planning for Change

The first concept to understand at the onset is that the business environment will change over time and probably more quickly that one would think. That's why I suggest to owners to plan for it. Keep track of the market. Monitor competitors. Introduce new products & services. Open new markets. Experiment with novel marketing techniques. The process I suggest is simple: OBSERVE, RESPOND, ADAPT, MEASURE

- **OBSERVE** - Look objectively at what is occurring, rather than focusing on the possible ways the business may be hurt. Take notes. Explore the landscape. And become a good detective by separating facts from guesswork. Talk with other owners in non-competitive geographies and see what they may be doing. This action is intended to collect as much pertinent information about the topic as can be assessed.

- **RESPOND** - Prepare an internal assessment report that justifies the reasons for the observation. Detail the reasons strategically, tactically, and financially. Approach the response as if you were providing it to an independent Board of Advisors for counsel. Include the justification for investment, retrenchment, sale, acquisition, or whatever the applicable solution may be. This helps you commit to the change regardless of how difficult it may initially appear.

- **ADAPT** - Here's the action step. Make the changes in small steps. Set big goals but stay grounded in reality. Watch for small steps of progress towards the end goal in your response. Remember the saying; Rome wasn't built in a day. People can smell a trumped up or artificial reason for urgency. Be firm, methodical, consistent, and caring.

- **MEASURE -** Measure your progress. Engage others in the change process metrics. Allow others to set their goals and help them analyze the impacts of their efforts. Be realistic about metrics because motivation can be dampened by unrealistic goals. As the change rolls out, encourage those to check in on progress regularly and make sure you are visible as the sponsor part of the engagement process. Over-communicate and frequently.

And then start the process over again. The key here is for the owner to never, ever, think they know everything about their business world. Customers will change. Competitors will change. Technology will change. Government regulations will change. Nothing in business is certain other than change. None of what was done yesterday, no matter how successful, is guaranteed to work today.

Two good books that address these issues are Jim Collins' _How the Mighty Fall_ and my co-author Bob Everett's book _The Entrepreneur's Guide to Marketing_. Collins provides an excellent discussion of how even highly successful companies can sew the seeds of their own destruction. Bob's book is an exceptionally clear primer on entrepreneurial business and marketing strategy.

Preparing for Transition

The second way to break the cycle is to plan for ownership transition while the business is still at its most valuable. Some changes are too sweeping or too sudden to anticipate. For business owners, these changes may also include health issues or family issues that can compel the owner to step out of running the company. There will be more about these issues later in this chapter. Nevertheless: PLAN, PREPARE, PREDICT, PERFORM.

- **PLAN** - Take the time to plan out the impacts of an exit or business transition. That includes understanding the people, products, services, timing, and markets for what you do and why your business exists. Study any specific industry information that is available on transitioning a business.

- **PREPARE** - There are many resources for preparing to sell or preparing to grow. Talk with professionals. Get a sense of time required to get to market that includes packaging. Get a sense for what can be done to maximize the value of your business. Put a stake in the ground with a valuation two years or more prior to your preferred exit date and clean up the financials.

- **PREDICT** - Talk with a professional intermediary and business advisor to discover what businesses like yours have sold for and in what time frame. Get real about the value you can expect your business to have in the marketplace and why someone would want to pay what you will be asking. Then try to predict what options there are for upfront cash, longer term installments, and continued revenue streams as part of the business sale.

- **PERFORM** - Operate the business with renewed enthusiasm because you have a Plan, are Prepared, and can Predict your future. Stay focused on building the business during this time so you drive profitability (and your multiple). Remember, if you are getting 1.5X to 6.0X to 10.0X cash flow, for every dollar you can improve cash flow, you will get back that many fold.

These simple actions place you in a position to succeed while transitioning. The essential message here is that exit strategies must be taken extremely seriously and planned for as far in advance as possible. Owners need to understand that there is a lot of misinformation out there about what you need to do when you leave a business. Therefore, GET A PROFESSIONAL TO HELP!

❖ ❖ ❖

Chapter 7: Business Advice Killers

❖ ❖ ❖

Introduction

It would be wonderful if Advisors could do their analysis and owners would simply do as advised. I have never seen it happen. In advisory situations, owners are uncomfortable, even afraid. They want to be sure that they are doing the right thing. In this chapter, I will discuss owner resistance and a number of the ways that the advisory process can go wrong. The purpose here is to alert both owners and advisors to these potential dangers so that they can be avoided.

Why Owners Resist Advice

There are a host of reasons why an owner may resist. But let's start out first with the dilemma and paradox of ownership. By their mere position as an owner, it's just *expected* that an owner is responsible for having all the answers. After all, it is their money and time. That couldn't be farther from the truth. The dilemmas faced by owners start with their belief system, in particular their "limiting beliefs." Limiting beliefs are the judgments we make about ourselves and our situations that limit our capability to act.

Ego

Our ego has a way of tricking us any time we go to solve a complex problem. There's a little voice in our head that makes a statement and then asks a question,

- **"I've done it before, why shouldn't I be able to do it again? Why would someone else be able to do it better?"**

I've seen this do-it-yourself, John Wayne attitude in many successful owners. However, that attitude only works when the situation is the same as it was at some time in the past. And nothing in the business world ever stays the same. In fact, some of the biggest changes in the business world are occurring in the current economic climate.

- **The ego also has difficulty accepting the possibility that someone else might be as capable as the owner is in the owner's own business.**

As I stated previously, I presume that the owner knows what they are doing technically. Otherwise, she would not even *be* in business. The Advisor's role is to help with decision support as a guide so that the owner can overcome her present difficulties and *stay* in business.

- **Many owners go into business for themselves because they believe they know better than anyone else.**

In many ways, mostly in the areas of technical or industry-specific knowledge, they do know better than others. It's quite possible that the owner's technical know-how was what initially allowed them to get into business. But ego prevents them from understanding what they don't know. And what they don't know can be very costly.

Bad Experience

Another reason some owners avoid retaining an Advisor is the axiom, "Once bitten, twice shy." They, or someone they trust, may have had a bad experience in the past and the bitterness of the fleecing is not fleeting. Unfortunately, there are a lot of people out there pretending to be Business Advisors who do not know what they are doing, and those people make it more difficult for those of us who are motivated to help and competent and qualified to do so.

For instance, I had engaged a husband and wife team of consultants in my office technology days when bringing on a new product line. I wanted to build a sales force quickly and their pitch and direct industry experience lit my interest, so we hired them for twenty thousand dollars and three weeks. Unfortunately, their "work" and "teachings" were fundamentally more about snake oil than results. I ended up shipping their green books back with a nasty note. I realized that I had been taken, and vowed never to hire a consultant again. Through that humiliating experience, I also learned to outline what I wanted as the basis for a consulting engagement and how to evaluate future consultants. The lesson:

Beware of the canned solution when your pain is great, because a deal too good to be true, generally is.

Just because an owner may think the Advisor was not worth the investment does not mean it is true. It is much easier to calculate what the Advisor costs than it is to calculate what the benefits are. This is especially true in cases where the Advisor provides a simple solution to what appeared to be a very difficult problem or where the benefits of the advice are realized over a long period of time.

That one bad experience didn't stop me from hiring a consultant to start up a temporary personnel service, or engaging technical consultants in our software business. What it did teach me was *how* to engage a consultant and furthermore in later years, a trusted advisor when I wanted self-development. I have enjoyed a 25 year relationship with that Advisor and will continue to have him in my life indefinitely.

Ready, Fire, Aim

Business owners tend to be people of action. In general, they would rather DO than think about doing. Hiring an Advisor to help think through a situation before taking action can seem like a waste of time and money to an owner facing a crisis and in a hurry to resolve it.

> **INSIGHT:**
> *We cannot afford to change if we want to keep things the same.*

I Can't Afford It

The final overwhelming source of resistance is that business advice is a luxury and the business cannot afford it, especially when things are not going well. There's too much economic risk. This is the old roof repair paradox. When it isn't raining, a leaky roof is not a problem, so it doesn't get fixed. When it's raining, it is too risky to climb up onto a wet roof to fix it, so the roof doesn't get fixed. Therefore, the roof never gets fixed. The long term problem is that below the roof the house starts to deteriorate from the water and eventually the cost will be vastly higher that the fix would have been.

It's also impossible to measure what a return on an investment in a Business Advisor will bring when the problem and solution haven't been fully defined.

As a business owner myself, I understand that cash flow is king. I preserve assets and preserve cash flow for clients every day. When talking to troubled business owners, I ask, "Can you afford NOT to get some professional advice here?" "What are the negative consequences of continuing to do the same thing and getting the same results?" "What are the risks of making a big mistake at this critical time?" If I have not quantified the potential risks and rewards, I have not provided the owner a complete proposal.

The advisory service is one of calculated risks for an expected return. In a recent engagement, I helped the owner sell a profitable portion of a business and close the remaining portion so the owner could retire.

In that engagement, I returned more than seven times the investment the owner made in me in additional negotiated savings and sale proceeds over what he had previously anticipated.

Advisory engagements are best viewed as an investment, rather than an expense. I have asked potential clients who do not have the money, if at all possible to hold off making major changes until cash flow allows them to engage me. That way, the risks of making big mistakes is lessened. In many of my complex engagements I have saved clients hundreds of thousands to millions of dollars because of the objective perspective I provided. Avoiding a catastrophic loss of a business that produces operating income, employs people, and provides an owner a living wage is my legacy.

Maintaining Control and Insecurity

Finally, owners may not wish to engage an Advisor because they do not want to feel stupid or out-of-control. An owner that feels that way is probably talking with the wrong Advisor.

> **While it is natural for an owner to feel some level of embarrassment if their business is having problems, it is not appropriate for an owner to indulge in those feelings by refusing help.**

Responsible owners have the courage to face the reality they find themselves in and marshal whatever resources are required, including professional advice.

A good Advisor is there to help with the owner's personal leadership development as well as with the immediate business problem. The right Advisor will make their client feel comfortable. They will strive to identify the best in each situation, not just the worst. If an owner senses arrogance, self-interest, or self-righteousness in a potential Advisor, he should throw that Advisor out of the office right away. That way professional, qualified Advisors won't get a bad rap.

Resistance to engaging an Advisor can be influenced by past experiences, fears of letting go, availability of funds, and a preference for action over reflection. But even in those cases of resistance, I have shown reasons why an Advisor may be an excellent addition to an owner's business assets.

Emotional Pitfalls

So far, this book has focused on the importance of advice in business and why it is vital for the business owner to leverage their emotional resources as well as those of the people around them. However, as with almost everything else, there needs to be a balance between leveraging personal strengths and indulging personal emotions.

Personal feelings can sometimes get in the way. Here are some of the ways:

- **Working IN the business, not ON it**
  Michael Gerber, in a series of books, discusses the danger he calls *The E-Myth*. Stated simply, the "E-Myth" says that if you can do the work, you can run a business doing the work. Gerber calls it a myth because it is commonly believed but is NOT TRUE. In other words, it is dangerous to think that just because you are a good cook, you are qualified to run a restaurant. So you must work ON as well as IN the business.

  All too often, however, business owners get caught up in doing the work, rather than managing the business. As any successful business owner knows, these are very different skills. When the management of the business is delegated to employees or, worse, not done properly at all, problems arise.

- **Micro-management**
  A common problem, especially among new entrepreneurs, is trying to control too much of what their employees do. Business owners sometimes think, often correctly, that they can do most jobs in the company better than the person they hired to do it. The problem becomes three-fold.

  1. First, micro-management almost always creates resentment in the employees being over-managed. It is perceived as a lack of respect and trust.
  2. Second, if the owner is always looking over people's shoulders, the employees are afraid to make mistakes and never learn to do the job well themselves.
  3. Third, it distracts the owner from the more important things she should be doing.

- **Hubris (Ego)**
  Hubris means that someone thinks that they are smarter than the people around them. They don't need to listen to others because they already know what is important. While people with hubris often come off as arrogant, arrogance is not an essential component. What is essential to hubris is being closed to new ideas and input from others. In *How the Mighty Fall*, Jim Collins argues that hubris born from success is the seed of the downfall of many great companies.

- **Getting too close to people**

  It is inevitable and valuable that business owners develop strong relationships with key employees. Trust, openness, patience, and acceptance are critical characteristics of excellent working relationships. Difficulties for the business arise when relationships become too close. I am not talking about "office romances" here, although they can create their own problems. I am talking about situations where truth and judgment are impacted for fear of damaging friendships.

- **Trying to do too much**

  The final pitfall I want to mention is over-extension. All too often, especially in the early days of the company, the owner out-works everyone else. This over-commitment and failure to delegate can lead to both fatigue and an inability to "see the forest for the trees."

Looking for Results in All the Wrong Places

Imagine going to a doctor's office with a fever. The doctor tells you that he can easily fix the problem and sticks you in an ice cold room for an hour. When he lets you out, he takes your temperature and "voila," it's 98.6. You're cured!

That sounds insane, doesn't it? You know that the fever is a symptom of an underlying infection and is not, itself, the problem. You are looking for the doctor to find out what the real problem is and fix that. When the problem is fixed, your temperature will go back down on its own.

Unfortunately, business financials are sometimes not thought of in that more rational way. Too often, business owners will make organizational or strategic decisions simply in order to make the short term numbers look better.

Let's take an example from Bob's former consulting experiences. (Neither he nor I were an Advisor there when the problem was created.) A particular company was suffering a decline in profits over two quarterly periods. Their bank was threatening to cut back on their line of credit if they did not show improved results by the end of the year. In order to drive up short term profits, the owner did three things:

1. Discounted their products in order to drive up sales
2. Slashed research and development in order to cut costs
3. Initially refused to engage a Business Advisor, also to save costs.

And guess what? Profits increased the next quarter. Was that a success story? Some would say it was. However, look at the long term effects.

- **First, the owner reset the expected price for his products by the aggressive discounting.** Once customers learn that you are willing to sell products at a lower price, the old price starts to look high. Large and long term customers will start to demand the discount price on an ongoing basis.

> **INSIGHT:**
> *When observations agree, interpretations may not.*

- **Second, by cutting R&D, the owner made his company more vulnerable to competition in the long run.** He also put out onto the job market people who had an in-depth understanding of the strengths and weaknesses of his existing product line: a treasure trove for competitors.

- **Thirdly, by focusing on moving the number rather than on hiring a seasoned professional to help diagnose the problem, the owner effectively "kicked the can down the street."** In other words, he just put the identification and solution of the underlying problem off until later.

There are a couple points to this story:

1. The first is that sometimes doing all the right things in the short run can create new problems in the long run. A good Advisor would have identified these potential problems and helped the owner focus on the underlying issues rather than just trying to make things look better.
2. The second point is that focusing on financial results, to the exclusion of all else, can create a whole new set of problems.

The Trouble with Numbers

Numbers are a vital part of any business operation. An owner cannot stay in business if the business is not profitable. The numbers, and by this I mean the standard financial reports (Balance Sheet, Income Statement, Cash Flow Statement), are also necessary for dealing with banks, taxing authorities, and, in some cases, vendors. A CPA should be able to guide you through the various requirements for financial reporting. These reports have accepted standards.

**However, it is critical that business owners
understand that numbers are NOT the
game. They are simply the
score of the game.**

Yes, balance sheets, income statements, and cash flow statements can reflect vital organizational functions. At the same time, these financial statements, like tax returns, present only a partial picture, and sometimes a skewed one at that, of what is actually going on in the company. Here are three reasons I say this:

- **Standard financial statements were designed to help assess taxes, not manage firms.**
  In the US, governments tax income and/or assets. There needs to be an acceptable, standard way to do this. If you have a job and a house, it's easy. The W-2 and 1099 forms tell the IRS what you earned and the local property appraiser tells the local government what your house is worth.
  It's not so simple if you are a business. The IRS taxes your profits and, under accrual methods, profits can be calculated in many ways. Even within General Accounting Practices, there are plenty of options for determining when income is realized, when costs are incurred, what counts as costs vs. what counts as investment, how subsidiaries are handled, etc. In recent years, there have been huge scandals surrounding accounting methods used by banks and investment houses. Perhaps the biggest example of how numbers can be configured for specific purposes in the accounting of the National Debt!

- **Standard financial statements were originally designed during the industrial age.**

  These statements do very well at accounting for plants and machinery. These have known costs and can be placed on standard depreciation schedules. In today's knowledge economy, however, setting a depreciation schedule for investments in technology or training for employees is simply guesswork, as is the asset value of intellectual property or a customer base.

- **Standard financial statements do not measure human capital, the "people value".**

  As I have talked about from the beginning of this book, personal factors or positive human assets such as passion, know-how, loyalty, ambition, tenure, networking strength, ability to execute, etc. can provide added value. As well dealing with any negative attributes such as manipulation, deviousness, vagueness and personalities can detract from business value. Yet these factors cannot be directly measured with financial statements.

The point I am making is that owners must not simply understand their financials, they must understand the reason that each number in those financials is what it is.

An Advisor can be very valuable here in working with the owner and her CPA to link operational and marketing issues to the financial results.

And finally, the owner must understand the intangible assets, liabilities, risks, and opportunities that do not show up in financials. As an example, a key intangible may be the strengths inherent to the management team. Additionally there may be off-balance sheet value such as a strong pipeline for future orders or time invested in developing the customer base as an expert resource for future product or market development.

Be Careful What You Measure

There is an old adage that states: "What gets measured gets done." That is certainly true with one slight variation: what gets done is what is necessary to reach the numbers specified by management. The more unreasonable or difficult people feel the target is, the more they will be tempted to fudge the number.

In my experience there is a corollary to the same adage: "ONLY what gets measured gets done."

This means that business owners need to be very careful about how they set numerical goals.

The point here is that "the numbers" are not something that can simply be done by an accountant and relied upon by management. These statements are certainly necessary for the government and for banks, but the savvy business owner understands that those same statements are vital, but insufficient to manage a company.

The Impact of Fear

In his book _Shine: Using Brain Science to Get the Best from Your People_, Dr. Edward Hallowell calls fear the great dis-connector. It can create a toxic work setting. It may work as a short-term motivator but in the long-term it destroys real motivation. Why? Because unmanaged fear creates unmanageable stress over long periods of time. It becomes unhealthy. People end up doing only what makes them safe, even when they know it is the wrong thing for the company.

A dose of short-term, healthy fear is generally manageable and can be good for the individual or organization to motivate right action, as in a sense of urgency. Fear can be corralled to be effective only if the fearful person feels empowered to do what is needed.

If fear is accompanied by disempowerment, arbitrariness, or randomness, it is disabling to both the individual and the company.

Fear also has to have a reason for living. It has to be fed by an underlying payoff for the individual creating the fear. For some owners, the payoff is that lower than normal wages can be paid. For others it's purely about control, and keeping people in the dark. For others, it's about feeding ego. Whatever the intent and payoff, we know

> **INSIGHT:**
> *Let go and others may hold on more tightly.*

that fear has been described by author Rush W. Dozier, Jr. as *"the quintessential human emotion"* and we need to be able to deal with it and balance its affects.

Fear comes from the Latin word *motere* , which means "to move." The word "motivation" has the same root. In the book: _Fear Itself: The Origin and Nature of the Powerful Emotion That Shapes Our Lives and Our World_, author Rush W. Dozier, Jr. states that

"Most of the problems fear causes in our personal lives arise from our failure to use the mental resources of the conscious mind to keep our primitive emotions in check....Even executives who are objectively in positions of great power and control, but nevertheless perceive themselves as to be at the mercy of events, are just as vulnerable to stress as their lowest ranking employee."

Hopelessness and raw vulnerability create unhealthy stress. Where stress is unhealthy, physical and mental illnesses develop. The body's immune system breaks down. If the fear is too intense and long lasting despair, depression, and/or addiction can occur. And the business fades into entropy.

Fear and the Downward Spiral

Personal issues really come to the forefront when a company starts having financial problems. When I am advising a company in trouble, the owner is usually feeling frustrated and angry. Under pressure, people typically fall back on what they are familiar with, what has worked before, or where they feel safe. In business however, that is usually not a good strategy. Businesses usually get in trouble not necessarily because of making bad decisions, but rather because they continue to act the same way after their business environment has changed. In other words, when things go haywire, management demands even more dedication to what got them in trouble in the first place! (See Jim Collins' excellent book *How the Mighty Fall* for an insightful explanation of this process.)

Emotions and anxieties typically run high in a turnaround situation. Things have been going wrong and changes need to be made. As David Eagleman states, *"There's a training period to rewire the circuitry of the brain to make a change. The correct training gets the right results."* However, I've observed situations where owners did not have the discipline to trust in the re-training process.

At the precise time they needed to stay focused, and allow the needed changes to happen, the fearful owner may "grab the wheel."

In a lightning strike moment, they break their competence circuitry and begin to meddle in the details of exactly how the changes should take place or, even worse, concentrate their energy on why things are not working as hoped. When this happens, the organization starts to lose the accumulation of learning and collective momentum towards any real progress. It's the same consciousness that took our surfers to fall off their boards.

The employees usually know what is happening. The owner's anger is often visibly targeted at one individual or group in the organization "who doesn't get it," and "isn't producing." Progress dies. Team members go silent for fear of retaliation.

The more the owner relies on employees only for "facts" and rejects their ideas and insights, the more those employees turn to placating and grousing.

They know they are just pawns in this chess game. There's only one voice left and that's the owner. Their hearts aren't in it. They keep their heads down to protect their jobs and hope the company survives. The best employees may seek work elsewhere.

The situation then becomes more about the owner and their anxiety, than it does about the progress of the business. It's a personal battle for control that isn't sustainable. And no one wins. The owner isolates. And the employees are "taught" by repetitive owner interactions that what matters is keeping their ideas and opinions to themselves and answering questions with the facts – just the facts – no more and no less. Like robots, they are directed with minutia that fills up their consciousness all day, and drains like water in a sieve at the exit door each night. The owner does not understand because logic won't get the desired result.

The same paradox unfolds: Once you begin to describe what it is, it flees conscious description.

Isn't that the description of situations when you need to tap inner courage? That means having faith when you don't have all the answers and believing that things will work out for the best.

Unfortunately, by meddling in the conscious, the emotional neural network that actually was sparked to make progress, for the right reasons, gets snuffed out by conscious detail. The only real decision maker now becomes fear. And business decisions that rely on fear drive insight away. That may have been a contributor to the problem in the first place, especially when the business is floundering. In most cases the situation was created by an excessive focus by the owner on certain specific details to the exclusion of other relevant information.

As Eagleman has outlined, *"Placing your eyes on something is no guarantee of seeing it. There is an illusion of seeing. The brain only sees small bits of the visual scene, not everything that hits your retinas. We have a natural blind spot."* We just seldom know where that blind spot is. The brain is making the changes. So it is with "blind spots" in business. The brain "fills in" the missing information.

Your conscious mind perceives what your inner brain tells you, not necessarily what is really out there. So just getting the facts isn't enough to solve the real problem.

As Advisors we see quickly that people's work often becomes more about appeasing the owner's anxieties, the flavor-of-the-day crisis of what he or she wants done, than it is in making any real progress. It's more about maintaining the owner's illusion of control than it is about organizational change and effectiveness. Ironically, the owner's ego may reinforce this position by asking itself, "How could I ever trust them? This team cannot operate independently without me."

It's usually at this point that the owner, who may have invested 25+ years in building the business, and who is suffering through a financial decline says, *"I want out. I'm tired. I want to sell."* Advisors with integrity then have to tell them the bad news that their business no longer has the value they once expected.

What happened here? The spirit of the business - the personal - was snuffed out. The people feel it. The owners are no longer getting what they want and don't understand why. In fact, it is difficult to explain it to them. It would be like speaking gibberish or a foreign language. We see the reflection in how people work and are connected.

The employees no longer feel safe, valued, or respected. They work each day for their paycheck. Being disempowered within the organization, they rely on a strategy of perseverance that directives will cease, hope that the situation somehow will go away soon, or they look for a new job. Customers, suppliers, investors, and lenders can usually tell that something bad is happening and start developing their own strategies for exiting the business relationship.

Unfortunately for our business owner above, in these situations, there is seldom any planning or preparation for crisis response to a major business problem or for an exit from the business altogether.

And what happens to fair market value in a death spiral? When a crisis occurs, the market value of the business takes a big hit.

As an Advisor, my first job is to break the downward spiral. That means getting the owner to be more open to the truth of the situation and getting the employees to be willing to continue their support of the company and its owner through the most difficult times. These are not business issues. They are personal issues. If I am to be at all effective, I must address them as such!

That is also pertinent to employee resistance. In a recent engagement, employees had been resisting doing compliance paperwork for several years. The company's internal workflow came under the scrutiny of an external insurance payer who elected to perform an audit. That audit resulted in extra fines, penalties, and reduced revenues to the business and shareholders. The president addressed the compliance aspects with the employees over two years, but they just refused to get on board. After absorbing audit fines for that period of time, the owners elected to dissolve the company. The employee resistance created an inertia that killed the spirit of the business going forward and they ended up losing their jobs. And the owners, who were unwilling to take the stern action that the employee resistance required, lost theirs, too.

The Impact of Inertia

**Many business owners tend to wait too long
when they are having a business problem.**

It may be out of ego or embarrassment. At times the problem doesn't hit the radar hard enough, especially if the effects are over a long period of time. Sometimes the owner just does not know who to turn to for appropriate advice. Instead, they tend to continue to do what they had been doing before perhaps focusing only on improving execution, hoping that somehow things will go back to the way they were.

**Few business owners experience crises as opportunities
for renewal. And that is precisely what crises are.**

I have worked with business situations described as hopeless, where the owners were afraid of losing everything, including their personal assets. As an objective Advisor, I consciously seek, identify and outline new, creative options that make sense. These are usually options that the owner has been unable to see.

**I have rarely been in situations where there weren't
two or three possible options to get out of the crisis
situation that the owner has not even considered.**

Once the owner sees that they have choices and makes a decision to act, much of the pent up fear, stress and pain start to go away. The focus shifts from problem to action.

I have also advised where the founder became terminally ill and I advised them in the selling of their business. It was a compassionate and heartfelt journey with the owner and family. And it encompassed many levels of preparation. To that end, in each critical care engagement I understand the level of energy and emotion required of caregivers and family members. Having cared for my own daughter during her bout with cancer, I understand firsthand that the effects of chemotherapy and treatments may also affect cognitive abilities.

> **INSIGHT:**
> *Lift others as they work and they will lift you in return.*

Whenever I take on an engagement like this, a succession transition or outright sale, I am fully vested in the power of the personal as an ally to the owner and his or her family members. I want to meet those influential spouses who have been behind the scenes but see many of the circumstances with a different lens.

Even in the worst of times, when fear can be at its highest, there can be a great deal accomplished when connection and positivity are made priorities.

In one of my engagements, a client had a prized franchise that he suddenly was faced with losing. After assessing what the problem was, I met with the staff and told them of the situation. I explained to them I had their interests first and foremost in my efforts and that I knew everyone had a family counting on a resolution. I reassured them that I had seen this before, and I honestly told them that there's no guarantee I could do it. But I promised my personal best and I confessed that I didn't have all the answers at the moment. Regardless, I vowed to do the best for them that I knew how. In return I needed them to help me and "take out their lamp from under the bushel basket for all to see" because it was obvious to our quality scores that we weren't communicating how much we cared about our guests.

I described to them my personal philosophy of the mind, the hands, and the heart of business. I told them our customers needed to *feel* their care. Our quality scorecard had been languishing. The unit was ranked in the bottom 5% for customer satisfaction. I asked them to do one thing for each of the next sixty days – smile. Smile at one another. Smile at the customer. Smile that we had an opportunity to make a change. Smile. Smile. Smile. Look at the guests and smile. It was a simple way to relieve the tensions I knew they were feeling and a way for them to positively contribute every day.

The story ends happily. We did get the franchise renewal and we did save the portfolio. We had navigated an almost impossible transition from a point where we were faced with losing the franchise in two weeks. I negotiated an acceptable re-organization and re-license between the Franchisor and the owners. And we saved $10 million in owners' *net portfolio value*. But as importantly, I kept my promise to those employees and the families that relied on that asset for their livelihood. Today they are climbing the ladder of performance and making progress towards the top half of the ranking for that chain.

Creative and critical are two sides of the same situational coin. Both conditions require developing realistic options that can be executed in business.

Some of the most profound and remarkable business transitions have occurred where there were previously unforeseen options.

By injecting the power of creative option assessment, the fear that our clients are experiencing is addressed head on. That's precisely how it works. Dozier comments that, *"Fear is designed to be self-correcting, to turn itself off by motivating us to take the appropriate action."* He further makes the point: *"We turn off fear by doing something about it – fight or flight. I'd worry that if the person would not respond to fear, that he was in denial,"* or as Dozier describes it, *"unspoken panic".* So the next time you have a fear, consider what the message is for taking action. I like to ask: what's the payoff?

The Impact of Other Blockages

There are a host of other blockages I can describe that hinder how personal factors work in the business world. They include overthinking, being stuck in history, a misfit role, obsession with logic, a focus only on data, over-rationalizing, and blame to name a few. These other blockages yield the same results – an obsession with control, or the lack of control, frustration and depression.

It is up to us to take accountability for our actions and therefore reason through these blockages and seek positive solutions that yield positive benefits. Most times there's a payoff for having a blockage in the first place. It may be attention-seeking, control, anger, aggression or irresponsibility. One must find the payoff to understand the blockage. I've had the occasion to work for or with several personality types that are difficult to make any real progress with on a personal level due to their traits. As is common with any behavior, they exist in shades of gray, but it is noteworthy to mention for you to understand them:

- **Self-centered** - These personality types generally tend to blame others for what is going on (or not) in the business. There is a pattern of a lack of empathy and or lack of feeling for anyone other than themselves. It is difficult for the self-centered individual to be reflective. Many times these are very intellectually-gifted people. However their "wiring" may be counter-productive to making any real change.

- **Roller coaster** - These personality types are hot and cold, high and low and may be inconsistent with direction or outright contradictory from one moment to another. It may be difficult to count on these personality types for decision support or to lead a change process.

Trying to understand these two types may be difficult without the help of a professional in Human Relations or Cognitive Psychology. The main point of my simplified description of personality type behavior above is that you have an awareness of these blockages for generating real progress during a transition or for developmental growth during transformation.

The blockages described above make it difficult to develop trust. And for Advisors, trust is the only bridge to transformation.

❖   ❖   ❖

Chapter 8: Making Advice Work

❖ ❖ ❖

Introduction

Business advice can have a profound and lasting benefit or advice can be given and received with little or no impact. Only when advice is adopted do benefits become realized as the business adapts to its new circumstances.

In order for transitions to occur successfully, the adoption of business advice needs to include each and every person involved with the business who has a "stake" in the final results, starting with the owner.

In this chapter, I discuss many of the practices that I have developed to maximize the probability that my advice will be successfully adopted and implemented. These practices have been applied in combination, in parallel, and sometimes independent of one another. They have been utilized as needed, depending upon my assessment of circumstances in each unique case. Therefore, I want to qualify my reader's expectations of this chapter.

While I can point to these practices as a critical part of each transformation I led, the process of applying and developing each practice has taken time and experience. Deciding when to apply a particular practice is up to the judgment of the Advisor and, sometimes, the owner. Without advisory-related experience these practices may or may not produce the desired result.

It's no different than my attempting to replicate Warren Buffett and his Berkshire Hathaway methodology for company value analysis and expecting to pick the same percentage of winners. Evaluating the same investment, I may have the same facts, and I may even have the same models. What I lack is Buffett's experienced intuition and insights based on the thousands and thousands of other companies he has evaluated. Therefore, the same facts may not necessarily be interpreted by Buffett or me in the same way.

And so it is with the practices I outline below. As an Advisor, I have learned what I can expect from the application of these practices because I have worked extensively at the craft of developing them. My concern would be that if you are in a critical business transition, you may want to have more reassurance of a positive outcome than trial and error associated with do-it-yourself practices.

Leading Change

Any successful change effort must be led by the business owner. Without that leadership and commitment, anything the Advisor attempts will be considered to be "optional" by everyone else involved.

Here are the Change Leadership practices of an owner that I believe are instrumental in making significant change possible:

- **Leading With Heart** - Obtaining minds, hands, *and hearts* of those involved in the change process.

- **People First, Always** – Everyone involved needs to understand the potential impact that changes will have on them personally. When secrets are kept by management, workers usually assume the worst and may become actively resistant.

- **Relying On Others** – There are always more people involved in any change than there initially appears to be. It is critical to appreciate and leverage that interdependence.

- **Relying On Strengths** - Everyone needs to be working with their strengths. The middle of a critical change process is no time to be correcting individual deficiencies.

- **Achieving Engagement** – When people are included in the process and understand why things are being done, they become supportive. Otherwise, the best you can hope for is compliance.

- **Building Momentum** – People's support is built over time. All initial successes, no matter how small, need to be recognized.

- **Measuring Progress** - Step back to measure direction and financial impacts of change.

What I recommend is that if you are interested in applying the above practices, visit my author's website, www.davidwimer.com. The site also has several ways you could enlist me or my firm as a guide in your transition and transformation project.

Leading With Heart

Whenever I lead a financial change effort, I make sure to communicate my beliefs and goals to a general assembly. In one particular case I had eighty-four people in a distribution and processing business. The business had been floundering under a prior leader. The founders had retired three years earlier and an internal successor with much industry experience had taken over running the business. The remaining corporate investor was experiencing a succession plan gone badly. In three years of under-performance, the business had produced a downward slide of profits into negative seven figures.

I accepted this particular assignment knowing that I needed to both "raise the bridge and lower the water," an unusual two-fold change process that would need to increase sales revenue with margin compression, and significantly reduce operating cost structure. I knew it would not be an easy transformation. A few weeks after my initial on-site assessments, I wanted everyone to get the same message at the same time, to grasp the same plan. At the general assembly and with the fervor of a mid-summer night's preacher, I simplified business change to three simple actions that were easy to understand and remember:

In order for change to occur, I wanted *their minds, their hands and their hearts* in the business - every moment, every day.

I promised that if we did so as an organization, we could succeed at changing the business. That's when I could feel the energy starting to spark, as people began to identify personally in their own way, with the vision of change and care for their future I shared with them.

Furthermore, I explained that

- **If we only used our minds**, and didn't act with conviction, the changes we wanted to make in the business would not be seen or felt by our customers and we would fail.

- **If we only used our hands,** without mind and heart that we'd be the busiest we could ever be. But we'd end up on the road to nowhere spinning our wheels. And

- **If we only used our hands and heart,** but didn't engage our minds, using common sense as our compass, we would end up lost again.

Most importantly, I outlined that *if we put our hearts into the business*, our minds and hands would follow. We needed to take the risk of doing things differently, experimenting, making mistakes and potentially looking silly being vulnerable. By putting ourselves out there for our customers to reconnect, we could reshape the business. And if we did this, we would reach our destiny and dreams.

By using our minds, hands and heart, we would take the right actions for the right reasons and would succeed. We would internalize our purpose and mission.

I reinforced my concept – mind, hands and heart – over and over and over again, whenever the opportunity arose. And what do you think started happening? The miracles of change quietly started to appear as individuals and teams were commenced to work on solutions while still running the day-to-day of the business. Eventually costs were lowered and sales rose. Margins were preserved, unprofitable customers chose to leave us and we worked our way out of financial difficulty over twenty-two months. Later, the business was sold. The successor I had groomed to replace me, and who was overlooked in the original succession plan, navigated the business to the finish line of a sale with a profit. It was a remarkable success story.

I want to make an important clarification. I'm not suggesting that business owners start ignoring the mind and hands of the organization. My point is that the minimum acceptable score is 3 out of 3:

All three elements, *mind, hands, and heart*, must be engaged before real progress is made in any business.

This model of mind, hands and heart became the foundation for my work in adapting to change and in the adoption of advice. By enlisting peoples' minds, hands *and hearts* I found any transition or transformation in business was possible. And as you'll see I believe deeply in the power of the people who are working in the business every day to make extraordinary contributions.

People First, Always

People are the primary conduit by which business operates. People are the spirit of the business. People shape culture. People create and follow process. People innovate or resist. People show respect and dignity in the workplace or express their personal biases and frustrations. People connect with customers.

People are the key to business greatness.

I have never seen a business that utilized even a fraction of the intellectual and emotional resources available within its people. Perhaps because it is obvious, too close, or in a blind spot, business owners fail to utilize people as an available resource for change. In learning organizations, (which we will save for another book), one of the key ingredients is that people have a passion for knowledge, understanding and trying new things.

Hidden inside people in a business, including the owner, is a huge untapped potential for problem-solving, innovation, and options.

Within every company I have ever worked, there were creative problem-solvers and unconscious option-seekers that the owner never even dreamed existed. They were right there in the business, and the secret is:

**It costs nothing extra to harness the powerful
resources of people.**

People want to give their personal best and owners desirous of making change need to explore how to mine their value. The message of people first, always is: adopt an attitude of abundance and a belief in untapped potential. The people in place can deliver more than one can imagine. Allow them to become a key part of the change process. Owners can then rely on them to help carry the business through any transition.

Relying On Others

Business owners do not like to be dependent because of potential vulnerability. The very nature and existence of an owner is due to their self-image or internal needs for self-dependence and independence. That's likely why they started a business in the first place. However, what initiated the start of the business may not help it stay in business. When the business becomes more than one person, expectations change. And that can become frustrating, unless an owner understands that being in business means accepting interdependence.

I liken interdependence to a "partnership" between owner and employee.

Interdependence is an important concept to successful business ownership. Wikipedia's dictionary defines interdependence as "a relationship in which each member is mutually dependent on the others." The concept of interdependence is that one person relies upon the other to fulfill certain commitments. Earlier in the book I referred to this reliance between Advisor and owner as a "duty of care." The same duty of care exists between an owner and her people in holding one another's best interests at heart.

> **INSIGHT:**
> *The more you lead, the more others follow.*

The owner and employees are interdependent which means they rely on one another.

People are a business' major asset. A job is a person's major asset. Each depends on the other in important, rich, complicated, and very personal ways. When the partnership is based on mutual respect and trust, it flourishes. When either party breaks that trust and acts to take more for themselves at the expense of the other, then the partnership dies and the business goes with it.

Think about this for a moment. It is very unlikely that an owner creates a business alone. There usually are explicit or implicit commitments from a lot of other people including:

- Employees
- Lenders
- Investors
- Suppliers
- Partners
- Customers
- Family members

These people, known as "stakeholders," may have given time, money, emotional support, legal commitments, and/or given up other opportunities to work with that owner. Each of these stakeholders relies on the owner to honor her commitments to them. And the owner also relies on the stakeholders to fulfill their commitments to the business.

Some stakeholders have bet their careers and their family's welfare on the company. This is a big responsibility for the owner. But stakeholders also have a responsibility to deliver on what is expected of them. The level of this duty of care to one another and reliance of both the owner and the stakeholders on one another grows as the business grows and expands.

The benefits of successful change cannot be realized unless the owner and his people understand the concept of interdependence. When the business faces a difficulty, asking for help can be a vulnerable decision for any owner. However, getting everyone engaged as we shall see later is valuable. Applying common sense to disclosure is appropriate, depending upon the transition at hand. It's also where a Business Advisor may become an invaluable resource.

**When business owners feel the most alone, vulnerable or
dependent is generally when they isolate themselves
or their thinking and limit their potential
for options and solutions.**

At these moments of turmoil with pressure mounting, an owner can easily feel overwhelmed. And the owner may ruminate and suffer the isolation of being the owner. But that aloneness doesn't have to be for long. When the owner can rely on others, inside or outside the business, as advisors to help navigate through her aloneness, much of the personal stress is eased.

Relying on others means when one wins, everyone wins. Viewing the adoption of advice as an interdependent duty of care to one another allows everyone to concentrate on their own role in the transition, providing options, solutions, possibilities, and best efforts at every stage.

Relying On Strengths

Relying on strengths means knowing who is capable of doing what. When leading a change effort, I want the internal leaders and change agents to work in the areas of their strengths. This will reduce costs, reduce management efforts, reduce error rates, and reduce the time needed for results.

In my early work I relied upon my own assessments of people's strengths using interview techniques and my intuition. Later, I found that utilizing a standardized instrument to evaluate strengths was much more efficient. Additionally it validated my intuitive insights. I recommend that even if you are not contemplating a transition or are not in a transformation at the moment that you explore these resources.

Strength assessment is a key resource to any business owner where having that knowledge applied can boost business performance.

I want to defer here to other experts in business strength assessment. I'm sure these are not the only references on strengths available. However, these are two resources I have personally used as an Advisor and have recommended to others to use. They are:

Kolbe.com – *And the 35 year work of Kathy Kolbe on conative (instinctual) strengths of the individual and the research of The Center for Conative Abilities. Kolbe provides standardized assessments and an understanding of the natural strengths we are born with to use. (kolbe.com)*

Gallup® StrengthsFinder® - *Based on study of two million people over a 25 year period identify the most prevalent human strengths in the Internet-based StrengthsFinder® Profile as more fully described in the book: NOW, Discover Your Strengths by Marcus Buckingham & Donald O. Clifton, Ph.D. (gallupstrengthscenter.com)*

Both assessments help to qualify where people may fit best in the business and how people may perform more utilizing their strength potential. For now, the takeaway is:

Always work on strengths and complement weaknesses.

It is exponentially more valuable to the business to bring people from good to great than it is to bring them from bad to mediocre or even from mediocre to good. When adapting to change, people working in areas of their strength build a confidence that is unmatched. Momentum builds more quickly. And likewise, insights for options, solutions and possibilities present more quickly.

The next practice is to understand the role of connectedness during the change process in achieving engagement of the entire organization.

Achieving Engagement

One book in particular imparts the importance of connection in business quite clearly: _Shine: Using Brain Science to Get the Best from Your People_, by Edward M. Hallowell, M.D. Hallowell states,

> _"Connection is the most powerful tool we can use to bring out the best in others and ourselves. In contrast, disconnection in the workplace may be the single most preventable, detrimental force that leads to under achievement, depression, disloyalty and job loss."_

Connection is the glue that binds people emotionally to their performance. I call this act of connectedness: Engagement.

When people are *engaged*, they have their hearts in the business and seem to be in a timeless state, focused on the task at hand, no matter how insurmountable it appears. They feel and believe that they are a part of something larger than themselves.

When people are engaged,

- They believe that people they like and trust are relying on them to come through.
- They believe that someone is looking out for their best interests.
- They produce better results.
- They feel motivated from positive reinforcement for the behavior that's valued.
- When asked to help, or their opinions and input, they feel valued.
- When something good is noticed and communicated, they feel recognized and appreciated.
- They want and respond to consistent, regular feedback and over-communication.

Engagement is sparked in individuals and groups when their leader believes they can accomplish something. It's the report card concept of starting out with an A and then working to keep it. Confidence is built when positive contributions are noticed and recognized. Recognition instills a sense of appreciation. I have seen the ordinary line worker transform into an extraordinary contributor during a business crisis based on these practices. Nurturing potential draws out the best in people to achieve extraordinary results.

**Engagement is an emotional process of getting
everyone connected and focused "all-in"
during times of business complexity.**

It takes an emotional sensitivity and commitment to be engaged and in the frame of mind of positivity and creativity. As an Advisor, I want to surround myself with that "feel good" energy even in intensely difficult circumstances. In fact, I believe it brings out the best in people and their actions, and it brings out the best in me as an Advisor. I can find something good in the strengths of any person and in any situation regardless of how dire. And I can find ways to address boundaries and correct behaviors without disrespecting anyone who wishes to remain stuck in negativity.

Building Momentum

It's my observation that every business has a unique, collective personality that's formed over time based on mindset and how people in the business feel. Some may think of personality and describe it as culture. I mean personality as an emotional quality, the essence of a business that one feels. If we are open, we can generally feel that business personality when visiting, working in, or working with a company. We either like it, or we don't. Quite typically the telling exchange is how we are treated as an outsider. And that interaction speaks volumes as to what is going on internally within the business.

**The business' collective personality is an aggregate of the
beliefs and emotions of the people associated with a
company that shines through to the outside.**

On the negative side, personality can manifest itself as a sense of discouragement, even despair, which erodes productivity and morale. Personality may present as employee resistance, grousing, fearfulness to make a decision, or apathy. And negative personality traits may be heightened in a downward spiral of the business or crisis, when everyone is feeling the intense pressure of difficult financial circumstances. As I covered in earlier chapters on the science of advice, the emotional neural network drives the bus on decision-making. And in negative situations, the emotional reaction is to fight, flee, or freeze.

A business' personality stems from how people are appreciated, how their work is valued, and how that value is communicated to them. A business' personality starts with the owner. It is the owner who sets the pace for beliefs and standards within the organization. It is the owner who communicates responsibly and compassionately. Therein the business owner becomes a teacher in words and in deeds.

The business personality is a mirror of the owner, and is reinforced each day.

If we are taught to contribute in a safe environment, we will do so. If we are taught to mistrust and be untruthful, we will do so. If the owner is a leader with vision, we will follow. If we know the owner cares about us, we will give her our hearts, hands, and minds to our work. And so it goes. Whatever is practiced by the owner, the employees will practice, much in accordance with the mindset theory of Dr. Dweck.

Personality is the heart of the business. It is the emotional flame of passion and purpose that fuels action.

As the sponsor of change, an owner must consider the personality of the business and its emotional energy. Because the collective personality *includes* the owner, and is influenced by the owner, an independent, objective Advisor may be better at facilitating the building of momentum. The owner may wish to remain a part of the solution and be perceived by the followers as "the owner" and not necessarily the change agent. The emotional difference as interpreted by her people is:

"We are all in this together and it will take all of us to get out of this together." rather than "I'm feeling the pain, so I'm going to spread it around."

Understanding the business' collective personality (emotion) is critical to building emotional momentum for change and ultimately for the adoption of advice. When people feel safe, they respond by investing their minds, hands, *and hearts* in support of the needed changes.

The art of transformation is when the business' emotional state changes from victim to victory through: leading with heart, accepting interdependence, relying on people and their strengths, achieving "all-in" engagement and momentum.

The final practice is comparably the easiest one. It is monitoring the change process and measuring progress.

Measuring Progress

The successful adoption of business advice can be measured by observing the quantifiable financial impact. As discussed in

Chapter 6, a goal is of no use unless the owner has a reliable way of determining whether or not that goal has been achieved.

What is first necessary is to set the above practices in motion in a digestible timeline I call chunks. These chunks may also be called milestones, critical tasks, or gates. What is important is to address progress by assessing:

- **Priorities** – Depending upon the positive/negative consequence, which objectives have the most positive/ negative impact in a ranked order?

- **Momentum** – Are initial results being achieved rapidly enough to gain internal momentum and build confidence in eventual overall success?

- **Focus** – Are the goals, steps, and metrics of the change effort clear to everyone involved?

- **Flow/Resistance** – Is progress becoming easier and any remaining resistance fading?

It is important that everyone involved be able to recognize and appreciate the progress being achieved. Making sure that progress can be reached in a reasonable timeframe provides immediate gratification and increases confidence, motivation, and momentum. And over-communication makes sure that the messages of little victories are spread to encourage others in their engagement.

Measuring progress and having a communications feedback practice is where an Advisor or internal Project Manager can provide scorecards, news flash reports, or supporting communications to the business members, letting them know how things are going.

Engaging Stakeholders

Not everyone that needs to support the change effort actually works for the business. Customers, suppliers, lenders, and, on occasion, government officials may play critical roles in making required changes.

Working with people outside of the company presents certain special challenges. Among these are:

- It is hard to ensure confidentiality.
- Outside stakeholders have primary loyalty to themselves and/or their own organizations, not the owner's business.
- There is usually little the owner can do to deter non-compliance.

I have learned that the following practices work well:

- Gain alignment on the exact nature of the problem. Everyone needs to agree on what is going on, and why.
- Find the common ground where goals are shared between the parties.
- Always tell the truth. The outside stakeholder must trust both the owner and the Advisor.
- Present the benefits and costs of the changes from each party's viewpoint. The other party may have to explain the situation to someone else and, therefore, it must make sense from their perspective, too.

Making Advice Work

Each of the practices I have outlined in this chapter is instrumental in making transformation in business possible. What practices may be applied depends upon the complexity of the business circumstances. How accurately these circumstances are recognized depends on a professional assessment of the business and its unique set of conditions it faces.

To navigate and transcend negative circumstances, a business must adapt to the complexity and change in order to be re-vitalized. By engaging others in an interdependent partnership, every person in the business becomes an agent of change. Relying on others' strengths that are oftentimes hidden and untapped is a key to achieving engagement and in building the momentum for change. As waves of momentum crest, insights come to light as unforeseen options, solutions and possibilities for the journey towards renewal. My advice to business leaders is this: enlisting a trusted, professional Advisor makes the navigation through difficulty a rewarding experience -- personally, professionally and financially.

In the next chapter I will outline guiding virtues that are applicable to any Advisor or business owner throughout the journey of gaining insight and adopting advice.

❖   ❖   ❖

Chapter 9: The Guiding Virtues of Advice

❖ ❖ ❖

"We will not solve the problems of the world from the same level of thinking we were at when we created them."

Albert Einstein, *[German-born Theoretical Physicist famous for his Theory of Relativity]*

I stated earlier that being a business Advisor was much more about *who you are* than strictly what you know. This chapter delves more deeply into the "who you are" part.

> **The guiding virtues came to me as lessons taught
> by my mentors and while working through many
> critical and complex business and personal
> circumstances.**

I felt my life's work would be less complete and unfulfilled if I hadn't committed them to writing for other's use. These guiding virtues are the foundations for any business relationship, especially where trust, stewardship, leadership, and service are important. Each virtue has a universal application based on truth. And being true to oneself and to one's word are essential to living a virtuous business life.

The Guiding Virtues fuel the results I strive to achieve for clients. In this age of complexity, with rapid change and shifting circumstances out of our immediate control, the Guiding Virtues help me and the owners I work with navigate business transition. The Guiding Virtues are qualities that help us get through the fogginess of confusion, or through the pain we may be feeling. The Guiding Virtues are part of a culture of businesses that can sustain change over the long term.

They are characteristics that I believe are necessary to be fully engaged and living the Business Advisor and business owner experience.

I have grouped them by their teachers, the Four Mentors:

Fred: The Outdoorsman

- Adaptability – The flexibility to respond positively to unexpected changes in circumstance
- Compassion – The ability to put ourselves in another's circumstances without judgment
- Curiosity - The inner drive to explore, discover, and understand

Dad: The Financial Chief

- Accountability – The willingness to "own" our results without excuses or blame
- Humility – The understanding that our work is about the client and the truth, not about gaining praise for ourselves

- Integrity – The commitment to speak the truth as we see it and honor our word

Gene: The Entrepreneur

- Connectedness – The ability to allow others to share in the process
- Passion - The "fire in the belly" that fuels the purpose for our work
- Resourcefulness – The ability to identify and utilize assets in the environment that others may not see

Jeff: The Merlin

- Acceptance – The willingness to see things as they are and not as we would prefer them to be
- Contemplation – The discipline of thinking things through before speaking or acting
- Intuition – The ability to get past "conventional wisdom" to identify new options
- Patience - The knowingness that occurs from deep practice, reflection and observation

Adaptability

"It is not the strongest of the species that survives, or the most intelligent. It is the one that is the most adaptable to change."

Charles Darwin, [Naturalist and Publisher of Evolutionary Theory]

We all experience change in our personal lives. Some change we seek; other changes are thrust upon us. In business it is no different. It is how we respond to change that makes the difference. When we resist or deny those changes, we squander our limited energy. By confronting change head on, working through or around it, we can adapt, survive, and flourish.

Adopting an attitude of flexibility is critical to long-term abundance. As Advisors, we thrive in "foggy" environments, where the owner's personal experiences and skills may not suffice. Our role is to help guide the business towards clarity. We help the owner learn new skills and new ways of looking at their world so that the fog lifts and paths become clear.

When negative changes occur, I see many business owners wanting to return to "the way it used to be." So they continue to do what they always have done, hoping that the changes are temporary and will eventually pass. Or worse, they ignore the changes or hope the changes will go away. An even worse strategy under circumstances of change is to "go back to basics" and do even more of what no longer works!

What makes us so uncomfortable with change? Change and transition points in business cause stress on people and systems. Research has shown that even positive life and business changes create stress. Humans naturally seek comfort in predictability. In general, we want tomorrow to look pretty much like today. If we want excitement, we want to be able to choose when and where we get it: sports, skydiving, rollercoasters, etc. Most of us do not like surprises.

The silver lining of change is opportunity.

Change is very challenging and requires even the best of us to re-think and reinvent. It takes effort. The fact is that the organizations that most quickly and effectively adapt to change and leverage the opportunities that change creates, end up thriving. Companies that refuse to adapt to changes, die. All we need do is look at some of the giant corporations from the past (A&P, Bethlehem Steel, F.W. Woolworth) to appreciate this truth.

But if a company embraces the opportunities that business changes present and adapts to them while the competition denies and resists, that company will come out the winner. A good Advisor can help an owner through this.

> **INSIGHT:**
> *Nothing can stay the same forever, so transformation is always possible.*

Adapting is something that I learned to do with my Uncle Fred in the wilderness when weather suddenly shifted. There were natural consequences to something as simple as putting on or shedding a layer of clothing. But in my youth, I didn't realize that Fred would later be teaching me once again about adaptability, this time in more serious circumstances. In mid-2011, I learned that Fred, the man who had inspired my love of the outdoors, was terminally ill. The long bone in his bicep fractured when he leaned against his house while mowing grass. It was a freak incident that indicated something was terribly wrong.

The surgery to repair Fred's shattered arm revealed bone cancer. I visited with him after his surgery and he was upbeat and resolute. I knew Fred as a fighter, and he didn't disappoint. However, a CAT scan showed he also had abdominal, lung and brain lesions, which meant the cancer had metastasized. Fred elected Gamma knife and chemotherapy treatments. During his oral chemotherapy treatments, Fred collapsed at home and was hospitalized.

When I visited him in the hospital, Fred expressed trouble swallowing. Under general anesthesia for an esophagoscopy, the procedure revealed throat lesions. Fred was returned to his room intubated and in a drug-induced twilight state for comfort, while the doctors evaluated his condition. The equipment was helping him breathe, yet he was "awake" enough and appeared that he wanted to desperately communicate.

As I spoke to him I found that he could understand, nod, and point with his index finger. He became more frustrated with the awareness of his condition. Intuitively, I took Fred's hand and began to draw letters on his palm. I would repeat the letter, as we sought to spell a word. Fred would respond with a nod up for yes, and roll his head side-to-side for no to indicate what letter he wanted. Letters and nods started to gradually form two words – COLD HANDS. It was a message between Fred and my Aunt Jeanette – he wanted her "cold hands" to rub his neck. I had found a way to allow Fred to communicate under incredibly difficult physical conditions. We had adapted to our situation and innovated.

Compassion

"Not all of us can do great things. But we can do small things with great love."

Mother Teresa, [Albanian-born, Indian Roman Catholic Sister and Founder of Missionaries of Charities for the World Poor]

**Compassion is about seeking to understand another
person and their situation without judging them.**

Almost every time a business owner comes to me for help, they have a major problem. And almost every time, that problem is the result of something that they did or failed to do. The opportunity to justifiably blame them for the problem or think less of them because of the mess they have created is almost irresistible. But resist we must. If we cannot put ourselves in the shoes of that owner and appreciate the circumstances under which the errors were made, we can never help them.

> **INSIGHT:**
> *Understanding is the most effective tool for healing.*

Those we interact with get it right away. They instinctively know and can feel our empathy. It is the way we respond to them with patience, seeking first to understand them. It is how we approach someone with respect and sensitivity. It is the bridge to connectedness.

From a practical perspective, as Advisors, we need truth from our clients above all else. When people feel criticized, blamed, or judged, we get excuses, rationalizations, blame, or just BS. We cannot base our advice on such shaky ground. I continually remind myself that if I cannot feel compassionate toward a particular potential client, it would be unethical of me to take the engagement, no matter what the fee.

Given my background, it is actually quite easy for me to feel that compassion. I have been in their shoes. I have seen years of hard work turn to dust nearly overnight. I have suffered through disputes with long-term, trusted associates. I have made some great decisions and some decisions that, in retrospect, make me cringe. In short, I have no standing to pass judgment on anyone else, especially another business owner.

What I have learned to do is to take responsibility for the mistakes I have made and learn from them. I can't imagine an Advisor who has not "been there" being of any real use to a client.

I've served business owners with terminal illness who needed to wrap up their affairs unexpectedly and without preparation. Nasty, ugly cards were dealt to them. And yet they were calm and accepting. In another case, where a family member was ill, the family wished to concentrate on being caregivers, and we helped to shepherd the business while they healed. Without compassion, we lose our natural ability to know what to do in these situations.

Sometimes, the best thing to do is nothing. Occasionally, I will just sit with a client in their sadness and misery and just talk through the moment. Sometimes I just take it upon myself to do as much as I can and carry on in silence, letting the client have some peace.

INSIGHT

It is difficult to separate my personal self from my business self. I don't want to. I see no purpose in it. I just want to be who I am and bring all my resources to whatever I do, personal or professional. I bring who I am to work. Everyone does. Some people just won't admit to it.

Some "gurus" teach that being compassionate in business is a weakness. It makes you vulnerable and other people will take advantage of that vulnerability. I believe differently.

I believe that in business, vulnerability is strength.

I apply it in negotiations that always end up more favorable to all parties than initially expected. In this regard, the strength in vulnerability also means being firm with boundaries and being victimless by choice. If someone is trying to take advantage of you, you probably should not be doing business with them. If you must, the awareness puts you on alert to watch out. At the same time, a failure to see the other side compassionately cements the adversarial nature of the relationship and makes it almost impossible to get beyond it.

Curiosity

"Life was meant to be lived, and curiosity must be kept alive. One must never, for whatever reason, turn his back on life."

Eleanor Roosevelt, [former First Lady of the United States and longest to live in the White House from 1933 to 1945]

Things are seldom what they initially appear to be. They are almost always richer and more interesting.

I am constantly amazed by business: the continual interplay of desires and beliefs, knowledge and ignorance, egos and dollars. And yet things still get done, albeit sometimes with more difficulty than is really required.

I want to know how business works. I want to know how my client's business works. I want to know how my client, him/herself, works. One of my reasons for this is practical. I cannot ethically make recommendations without an understanding of how those recommendations will play out. The other reason is purely personal. I am curious.

Growing up, I was one of those difficult students who always asked "why?" Answers like "Because I said so," "It's right here in the book," and "This is the way we do it here" never seemed to suffice. However, I was fortunate to have a Latin teacher, who took the time to encourage me. She certainly didn't have all the answers herself, but she did teach me that, behind the "school solutions," there was a fascinating world of unknowns and that was where the fun was.

She also taught me to trust my gut and to keep being curious and asking questions until I got that gut feeling that told me I was close to the truth.

This attitude has been a great resource to me in both my professional and personal lives. Way too often it seems that when faced with a problem, people latch onto the most convenient answer or the most comfortable one and immediately quit seeking at that point. Later (sometimes not much later), they find that the problem isn't solved and proceed to do that wrong thing even harder with the idea that they just didn't "try hard enough."

One of the mysteries in life is how we develop our interests and then how they may eventually be threaded into our careers. I had chosen a pre-law course of study in college that included two introductory accounting courses. The accounting mechanics were pure drudgery and caused me to re-think my course selection, a simple decision for the next semester. One course in particular held my fascination. I was curious. No one could have convinced me at that moment, that an easy decision about following my curiosity would have the power to reshape my life's direction. It was counter-intuitive to my training from athletics where I relied on setting a conscious goal and pushing myself to reach it. I had been taught that quitters never win, and winners never quit. Sacrifice of oneself in the service of the team was man's highest calling.

I didn't understand why this course of study attracted me. I followed out of an intense curiosity and allowed it to lead. I actually felt guilty about my decision to further investigate this giddy feeling and selfish alternative. However, what I learned was that this science had just the combination of elements to keep me glued to it – wonder and awe, coupled with statistics and analysis – the lightning sparks created by opposites of fact-finding and intuition. Like peeling an onion, I dug deeper and deeper into its core and found more and more of myself. What was this subject matter that carried me to my first job in business-to-business sales, through five start-ups of entrepreneurial business pursuits, key executive assignments of leadership, and work as an Advisor? Psychology.

Curiosity gives us the motivation to keep looking even when we initially think we know. It puts truth above expeditiousness or convenience.

It turns every new situation into an opportunity for wonder. It gives us the power that comes from a deeper understanding and appreciation of situations than most people have. And it's fun.

Yet curiosity cannot stand alone. If it did, we would all be like mad professors bouncing from one idea to another as our whims flow. To be effective, curiosity requires some discipline. We need to decide what issues we are curious about. We need to be able to distinguish what is relevant from what is trivial. We need to be able to tell when further digging would no longer be worthwhile. These skills come with time.

Accountability

"It is wrong and immoral to seek to escape the consequences of one's acts."

Mahatma Gandhi, [Leader of Indian Nationalism and lawyer; non-violent pacifism]

As I have said several times so far in this book, business advisory is a professional practice. Like medicine, law, or accounting, the client places their trust in us to do something of vital importance. However, unlike medicine, law, or accounting, there are no certifications, and no professional standards against which to assess Advisor performance. The client must totally depend on the Advisor to act honorably. This is one of the major reasons I am offering these guiding virtues.

One of the most critical of these virtues is accountability. As people, we are responsible for our actions. We are responsible for ourselves. As Advisors, we are responsible for providing the best, most insightful, and most informed advice we can. If we make a major error, a lot of bad things can happen in the client's business and that client has little recourse.

I live by the following standards:

1. Never promise more than you can deliver, either specifically or by implication.
2. Establish reasonable objectives that are clear, measurable, and written.

3. Don't keep secrets from the client. Discuss any problems or mistakes with the client as soon as possible.
4. Accept responsibility for results within your control. Don't blame others.

I am very careful to understand as much as I can about the nature of a potential client's problems and expectations before I take on an engagement.

I will only take on a client when I sincerely believe that I can help them and the client will accept my help. Otherwise, I walk away, no matter what the fee might be.

From the other perspective, clients need to be wary, too. There are a lot of people out there claiming to be Advisors, consultants, and/or coaches. Some of us have chosen business advice as a profession. On the other hand, there are others who may not have been able to find work, especially mid-career, and have taken on the consultant role as a last resort. Some of these people are very well meaning and may have had a great deal of business experience as an executive within a company. However, just like being a defendant doesn't make you qualified to be a lawyer, being an executive does not automatically qualify someone to be an Advisor. The owner needs to talk about experiences outside of the prospective Advisor's own industry in order to be sure that Advisor can deliver.

Setting reasonable objectives can sometimes be more difficult than it might at first seem. Typically, an owner hires me when they are in some sort of pain. They want me to help them fix the problem. What some prospective clients mean by that is that they want me to take over responsibility for the problem and be totally accountable for the result. This I cannot do. I can inform and advise but I cannot make the final decisions. That responsibility is solely the owner's. When explained, most owners understand this. If an owner is not willing to accept responsibility for making the final decisions, I walk away.

Whenever I can, I establish clear metrics for performance. Sometimes I must be a bit creative to define metrics that are actually related to the problem at hand and reflect the progress and changes that need to be made. Interestingly, these discussions about performance metrics usually lead to some of the deepest insights and understandings that develop during the entire engagement.

As Advisors, our product is truth. Our skill is discerning the truth amid chaos, pressure, hidden personal agendas, shame, and an ever changing business environment. We are not oracles, however. We have no direct access to divine wisdom. We use what we have to do the best we can. But if we were to lie or withhold essential information from clients in order to protect ourselves or the income we derive from the engagement, we would invalidate our essential value. That must not happen.

Finally, we stand or fall on the success of the client. While we cannot control owners, or anyone else for that matter, we must accept the results of our work without shame or blame. If we have been true to the client and to ourselves, if we have done our best to discover the truth, and if we have presented options in an open and understandable way, that is all we can do.

Humility

"Humility, like darkness, reveals the heavenly lights."

Henry David Thoreau, [American author of Civil Disobedience, poet and philosopher 1817-1862]

In today's pop-psych, feel-good world, the virtue of humility has been getting an undeservedly bad reputation. Humility fundamentally means that you do not place yourself above other people. The opposite of humility is arrogance, thinking you are superior in some way. Unfortunately, many people equate humility with humiliation, i.e., with self-abasement, shame, embarrassment, or dishonor. Nothing could be further from the truth.

> **INSIGHT:**
> *In our pursuit of more, we end up with less.*

Providing business advice requires true humility. We work for a client. It is their business, their money, and their goals. They make the final decisions. They reap the big rewards when the results of your work come to fruition. And they will take the public credit. The Advisor does the research, proposes ideas, assists with execution, and then steps aside. But the Advisor has the incredible experience of knowing that they made a difference in the lives of others.

In order to be effective, the Advisor must get their public ego out of the way. Otherwise, there will be a constant battle with the owner and key employees over who gets credit and who gets blame, over who came up with the great ideas, and who is responsible for successful execution. When the Advisor assumes an attitude of humility, no one else is threatened or offended. Resentments and resistance are much less likely to emerge. Truth is much more likely to be told.

Humility is not an easy virtue to develop or instill. Today's culture tells us to stand tall, be who we are, find our special talent, focus on our successes, etc. etc. We are our resume. Get into that great college, get your MBA, and intern at a Fortune 100 or international consulting firm. *"Show 'em what you've got. Win, Win, Win!"*

That attitude may work in some environments. It will not work if someone wants to be a successful business Advisor. The molding of a great Advisor comes, in part, from confronting their inner fears and failures.

Success does not ground a person. Learning from trying, failing, and getting back up does.

Seasoning occurs when a person learns to balance a keen sense of self, mission, purpose, and meaning, with the acceptance that occasional misery and failure will happen.

Many people only learn this as a result of an ego-shattering or life-threatening event. These events can break though self-delusions and, if the person is willing, lead to true humility along with compassion and authentic self-esteem.

> **INSIGHT:**
> *To get back on track, you may have to get off track.*

I was very fortunate to get my first big lesson in humility when I was quite young. As an adolescent in 8th grade, my angels were looking over me. I was starting to hang around casual drug users who were not a normal part of my circle of influence. My eighth-grade teacher was a nun who took notice. I was acting stupid and talking like it too. She asked me to take a walk outside the classroom, so we walked up to street level and onto the sidewalk outside the classroom. I felt embarrassed to be singled out. She suddenly stopped. I reactively stopped and looked up at her. I was 5'4". She was an imposing 6'1". In an instant she pushed me up against the block wall, grabbed my tie and pressed hard into my sternum with her fist.

She went nose-to-nose with me to make her point. I was in for a lesson that lasted a lifetime. She said few words. *"I want this nonsense to stop. You are who you associate with. Get yourself together. I won't allow you to throw away your mind."* That moment became one of the most significant emotional events in my life. I felt ashamed of my idiotic behavior. With fear as my ally, I agreed to change, and swallowed my pride. Here was a person who truly lived her vocation.

Looking back, I am humbled by her high personal commitment of care for me. She took teaching to heart and her intervention saved me at a crossroads in life.

In my business life, the loss of a bright technology company due to unforeseen circumstances was also humbling. I considered myself pretty street-smart. But reasoning alone didn't salve the blistering feeling of failure. I found that working for other business owners offered me time to gain perspective. With a healthy layer of humility, I was less quick to judge owners and others during my assignments, and more interested in finding the right actions that gained the best results. It stopped being about me and became solely about the work. I studied by observing. I found myself asking the right questions to understand complex business situations. Not surprisingly, when I got my ego out of the way, options and solutions started to flow.

From that perspective of humility, I immersed myself in developing my practice in the arts of turnaround, business finance, capital, investment banking, and debt re-structuring. These were disciplines I had not mastered until after my own company collapsed. I also honed my problem-solving skills as each assignment presented complex new challenges. I just *wanted* the learning experiences and they showed up naturally. My business education has been hands-on and not always pleasant. But the firsthand experience has been so valuable. And as long as I remain humble, I remain open to learning even more.

Integrity

"I am not bound to win, but I am bound to be true. I am not bound to succeed, but I am bound to live by the light that I have. I must stand with anybody that stands right, and stand with him while he is right, and part with him when he goes wrong."

Abraham Lincoln, [16th President of the United States]

Integrity is the foundation for any relationship in business. It's your word. In the end, it is all you have. Without integrity, you cannot build trust. Without trust, you cannot build relationships. And without relationships, you cannot build a business.

> **INSIGHT:**
> *We may not deserve a circumstance thrust upon us. However, it may deserve us to conquer.*

Integrity answers the question: *"Can others rely on me to do what is right, to do what I say?"* It means doing the right thing when it's not economically or personally convenient. It means doing what is right when nobody is watching.

We can only judge integrity by watching and observing the actions of others, not by words alone.

I take your word seriously. It's a promise or pact I can count on. If someone tells me they will do a certain thing, I acknowledge their desire, but most importantly, I watch their behavior. If words and deeds are inconsistent, I bring it to their attention. Why? Because I believe that integrity – counting on another to act in accordance with what they say – is vital to trust. If a person won't keep a promise to themselves, we don't have a chance to succeed together at work. Consistency fuels a mutual trust, which results in great work. I need to have trust. It's a "no budge" virtue. Never, ever break your word.

Connectedness

"Humankind has not woven the web of life. We are but one thread within it. Whatever we do to the web, we do to ourselves. All things are bound together. All things connect."

Chief Seattle, [Leader of American Indian Duwamish Tribe and namesake of the city in Washington State]

The ability to connect is what makes us human. The better we connect with others, the more successful we will be. People make their decisions for personal reasons. The more we connect, the better we understand those reasons and the more we can serve them.

> **INSIGHT:**
> *A gift is as important to the giver as the receiver.*

The ability to connect with customers is essential to a business. If a company competes on price, a competitor can always offer a lower price and take the customer. If a company competes on features, a competitor can always offer a "better" product and, again, take the customer.

> **But if a company can connect with a customer and offer
> a relationship based on respect, reliability, and trust,
> no one can take that customer away.**

The same thinking applies to employees, suppliers, investors, and other stakeholders in your business. One must give trust to get trust; give loyalty to get loyalty; offer personal connection to get personal connection.

An Advisor must be a master at connection. The Advisor's role is to help a business owner make decisions. If decisions are ultimately made for personal reasons, then the Advisor must understand those reasons or no effective advice can be offered. Similarly, if an Advisor cannot connect with people without bias, judgment, or agenda, then they will never get truthful, open information from suppliers, customers, staff, or anyone else.

Many of my past clients have remained friends long after our working relationship ended. Many of those have become part of my network of resources. It may have been a transaction or a transition that brought us together. But it is connectedness that keeps us in touch. Consider that many clients must share their deepest dreams and darkest concerns with their Advisor. I hear what keeps them up at night worrying. I may meet and interact with family members. I see their flaws and shortcomings. I also see strengths that they and those closest to them miss. One cannot advise unless you know their entire story without passing judgment.

Connectedness allows for the truth to be spoken - respectfully, gently, and compassionately.

Passion

"If you follow your bliss, you put yourself on a kind of track that has been there all the while, waiting for you, and the life that you ought to be living is the one you are living. Wherever you are—if you are following your bliss, you are enjoying that refreshment, that life within you, all the time."

Joseph Campbell, [American writer, mythologist and lecturer on mythology and comparative religion]

Passion is the internal fire that drives us to do what we do. It is an intense enthusiasm. It is what we would choose to do with our time and our lives, even if we had plenty of money. Passion creates energy. When we meet a person who has a passion for what they are

> **INSIGHT:**
> *Chasing success can cause it to run away.*

doing, we can tell. Passion can be infectious. Likewise, if the passion is destructive or mean, we feel uncomfortable or even a bit scared.

True passion for one's work changes everything. If one works for money and the money doesn't come, they can feel disheartened or discouraged. If one works for praise and the praise doesn't come, they can feel resentful or unappreciated. If one works for achievement and you don't reach your goals, they can feel like a failure.

But if one works because they love what they do, the money, praise, achievement, and other external criteria no longer serve as the measures of success for the work.

The work itself, and the enthusiasm for it, are enough. Interestingly enough, when someone has the passion, the other stuff generally shows up too.

As an Advisor, I serve from a place of passion. I commit to performing my best each time a client entrusts me with helping them guide their company. That passion helps me to relish difficult situations knowing that those are the times when my clients need me the most. That passion keeps me going enthusiastically when things get messy, as they always do at some point. That passion for the work allows me to step back when the job is done so the client can say they did it themselves. Yet, at the same time, they always know who made it possible and rarely quibble about the fees.

While passion can fuel determination, drive, and perseverance in business, it can also make us blind. Sometimes, the hardest thing for me to do in an Advisory engagement is to keep digging after I am convinced that I already have the answer. I want to get going, make the changes, and see the results, and I want it NOW! The client needs it NOW! It's more fun if I do it NOW!

That is why passion is necessary but not sufficient. It must be tempered by other virtues, especially curiosity, humility, and contemplation. Left un-tempered, passion can eventually lead to arrogance, inflexibility, and intolerance.

> **INSIGHT:**
> *Doing our best is only ours to know.*

As Advisors, we are seekers. It takes passion to seek the truth in all things. It takes passion to stay motivated and on tract during tough times. It takes passion to understand that the client comes first. And for us, it takes passion to be a great Advisor.

Resourcefulness

"Aerodynamically, the bumble bee shouldn't be able to fly, but the bumble bee doesn't know it so it goes on flying anyway."

Mary Kay Ash, [Founder of Mary Kay Cosmetics]

In his classic book on creativity, *A Whack on the Side of the Head*, Roger von Oech states that one of the biggest barriers to problem solving is putting restrictions on the solution that do not need to be there. He calls these "mental locks." Resourcefulness is all about identifying, overcoming, or just ignoring these mental locks.

Resourcefulness is a very useful quality in today's world.

It is the ability to find ingenious, enterprising, and creative solutions to issues that have left the business owner stuck. It is the ability to ignore conventional wisdom in the pursuit of solutions.

It is akin to being a treasure hunter. When everything is seen as a possibility or as a resource, it is possible to find gold where no one else thought to look. It is fueled by a spirit of wonder and adventure, and has the excitement associated with the hunt itself. Resourcefulness is an explorer's key skill for survival and for conquering new territories. Resourcefulness is an Advisor's key skill for overcoming a business' long standing problems and taking the business to a new level.

It is the art of improvisation. It can be utilizing a resource that has never been used before or never used in a certain way before. It can also be simple ignorance of the constraints that everyone else takes as given, e.g., the bumblebee.

I once worked with a company that believed it had maxed out its manufacturing capabilities. That had put a lid on its profits and the owner was not going to be able to get the price he wanted for selling the company. Upon a careful review of the company's operations, I noticed that it was only doing large jobs. They had a

> **INSIGHT:**
> *The more you focus on fixing, the more broken things you'll find.*

number of reliable customers and the work came in regularly without a great deal of marketing effort. What caught my eye was that much of the plant remained idle as the large jobs often only required certain skills at certain times. I advised the owner to look for new, smaller work in new markets to fill in the gaps. In that way, growth of up to 40% could be achieved without significant investment in equipment or staff.

The owner had been so focused on achieving excellence in his core business, he had never thought to stray outside of it.

While owners usually have good relationships within their industry including customers, suppliers, subcontractors, and sometimes even competitors, an Advisor can bring in a vastly larger network of resources. My network includes executives in many different industries, a wide array of specialist consultants, attorneys, accountants, academics, recruiters, and association executives. I belong to several

181

professional networking groups. I am tapped into literally hundreds of other professionals around the country that I can call on for additional insights. And I can do so discretely and confidentially.

The resourceful Advisor doesn't get caught up immediately in the specificity of one potential solution. Rather the Advisor utilizes their network as a brain trust to source multiple solutions. There is usually more than one path that could result in an acceptable solution. A skilled Advisor will use their resourcefulness to identify and evaluate as many of these options as possible.

Acceptance

"Grant me the serenity to accept the things I cannot change, the courage to change the things I can, and the wisdom to know the difference."

Reinhold Niebuhr, [Protestant Theologian of Christian Realism and author of The Serenity Prayer]

Situations are what they are. The only way to make things different is to take action and the effectiveness of action depends on an understanding of the reality of the situation. This is so obvious that you may be wondering why I even mention it. But many people refuse to deal in reality, preferring to maintain their biases, preferences, and illusions even in the face of overwhelming contrary evidence.

The problem is that few of us rigorously seek to understand the full truth of our circumstances and, when we do, we do so with a lot of emotion. It feels better to pretend things are different, or that we are not complicit in creating our present reality. But things are not different than they are and we are always complicit in creating our current reality. No amount of hoping, or wishing, or denial will change that. When we see things as they are, we are not fooled by the illusions supported by our egos and our fears.

I am not saying that everyone lies, although some people do. There is a natural human tendency to "look on the bright side" and "make the best of a bad situation." It is normal to try to see things in a way that does not reflect badly on us. Unfortunately, many of us also learn to be victims, blaming others (boss, co-workers, parents, the government, etc.) for our ills. That makes it easier emotionally. We ourselves are not to blame nor need we feel responsible for making things better.

**What really happens when we fail to accept things
as they are is that we give away our power.**

It is impossible to fix a problem if we have a false understanding of that problem and its causes. It is impossible to prudently manage or invest organizational assets if we pretend we have more or less than we actually have. It is impossible to satisfy customers and find new ways of serving them if we believe we already understand what they need and no longer have to listen to them.

> **INSIGHT:**
> *Change occurs when you get comfortable with being uncomfortable.*

The good news is that there is a powerful way to identify those areas where we fail to accept reality. Just notice where our resistance is. Are we reluctant to examine our monthly financial statements? Do we dread that customer meeting or that performance review we have to do? Is there something we do not want to discuss with our business partner or investor? Resistance can tell us where we need to look for the truth.

One of my favorite mantras is, *"Embrace what you most resist."* It's a way of acknowledging the inner struggle with resistance and acceptance. As humans, we wrestle with circumstances that are thrust upon us. In business, it happens all the time. We can resist and continue to push our way, or we can stop pushing, step back, acknowledge the resistance, and find out what is really going on. By embracing the energy of resistance and treating it with respect, we can start to ask the right questions. What's the message here? Why am I resisting this issue? What is my fear? Why do I fear it? Is the fear real or imagined? What are the possibilities for growth? What other options might I have at my disposal?

An unwillingness to accept reality also leads to frustration. Early in my career as a business owner, what drove me was a pride in accomplishment. Earnings were my only scorecard. It was a carryover from what I learned in my sales positions. But as a new owner I didn't understand much about management or business leadership. After suffering less than expected results in a number of sales initiatives, I had bankers climbing all over my back for details about why I had missed my projections. I needed to assess what was going on and where the problem existed. Was it my salespeople or me? I questioned why I gave opportunities to others who wanted less for themselves than I did. I would expect certain outcomes. The sales staff would agree to them. We would miss targets. I would be frustrated. They would feel badly. I would set new expectations. And the cycle would perpetuate.

What I needed to learn from those experiences finally exploded in my head. I wanted them to be like me, to have all the drive, motivation, and pride that drove me. I was unwilling to accept the fact that they were not me. I had no idea what motivated them or how their

> **INSIGHT:**
> *A shared vision is greater than a clear vision.*

motivations might fit with the work that needed to be done. I found that I was pushing myself for all the wrong reasons, and setting unrealistic goals for them and for me. They needed to set their own goals and I needed to accept them, strengths and limitations, for who they were. Once I understood that, I began to see my salespeople differently and we began to make progress. I learned that you can push all you want, and if the motivation is not there, the pushing is a waste of energy. When I realized I didn't have to push anything anymore, a huge pressure fell off my shoulders. And results that had previously seemed impossible started to occur.

One of the great strengths of an Advisor is the acceptance of reality. While a good Advisor cares deeply about their client and is passionate about making things better, the Advisor is in a position to examine the facts dispassionately, without bias, blame, or judgment. The only objective is truth.

As an Advisor, I must accept the reality of my client's situation and deal with it accordingly, even if they do not. By accepting reality, I can actually start the real work of finding effective options and solutions.

The paradox is that through acceptance, we find the answers we were trying to get through our futile attempts at control or delusion.

Likewise, an Advisor must understand limitations of a client's performance and accept them as truths. No client will accept the Advisor's judgment as law, nor should they. At the end of the project, the Advisor must accept the fact that it is the business owner that makes the decision and the decision may be "no."

As an example, I once sat down with an owner who wanted desperately to sell his business. He and his partners ranged in age from their late fifties to seventy years old. They had grown tired of operating a business that had little long term future as it was. There were no successors who could continue to run the business. They had drawn significant amounts of cash out of their business each year and needed to borrow operating funds just to feed their survival. Then along came an interested potential purchaser. The owner responded to an inquiry from this perspective buyer who at first blush was a strategic, ideal fit. The owner quietly confided to me that, "This is a slam dunk. A ninety-day close." Naively, I took the bait and reduced my contingency fee. Neither deal team acknowledged it, but the deal was dead after six months. The fantasy that there was a deal there lasted for four years. In the end, the seller acknowledged the reality that the buyer had no ability to borrow the money needed to consummate the deal.

The moral of the story?

Accept reality when you see it, and don't be fooled by the illusions of other people. Things rarely turn out the way you expect.

If we accept what reality delivers, even though we are disappointed, there may be a good reason. It just may not be evident right then. And many more times, whatever we initially thought as a loss, can turn out much, much better.

Contemplation

"What we plant in the soil of contemplation, we shall reap in the harvest of action."

Meister Eckhart, [German Theologian, philosopher and mystic 1260-1328]

Great decisions are never made in a hurry. They are not made in meetings. They are not made to reduce immediate fear or pain.

The best decisions are made in quiet reflection and contemplation of their costs and consequences.

Too often, we make important decisions while racing along the daily grind. We just want things to keep moving and so we respond rapidly to clear our plate. We are sometimes unaware of their impact until later. It is at these times that we may want to ask for a break – *"Can you wait until tomorrow? I'd like to sleep on it."*

> **INSIGHT:**
> *In the fast-paced world we live in, contemplation is not a luxury -- it is requirement.*

Allowing our minds, both logically and intuitively, to work through the full implications of a complex decision is essential. That may mean doing nothing, or doodling, or shuffling manila files around, or taking a walk, or playing a video game: anything that allows the mind to relax and provides time for the creative process to work through the decision.

**As Advisors or as business owners, we need to learn
how to assemble the facts and then have the
discipline to step away for contemplation.**

I find it interesting that in Western cultures it is considered to be inappropriate to interrupt someone when they appear to be busy while in Eastern cultures it is inappropriate to interrupt someone who is sitting quietly.

Decisions often have implications far beyond what we may first think; important decisions always do.

**What first appears as a simple decision may
end up causing a complex problem.**

Perspective comes from contemplation. Take a look on a clear night and see the stars. They can't be touched. They can't be felt. They can only be seen. The distances to them are calculated in light years, the distance the light travels in one year at 186,000 miles per second (about 5.8 Trillion miles). The nearest star is over four (4) light years away and the furthest star we can see is about 14 billion light years away. And, there are billions of billions of stars in the universe, more stars that there are grains of sand on all the beaches and all the deserts of Earth. Puts our little problems in perspective, doesn't it!

In the advisory relationship, each party needs to give the other the space for contemplation. Owners need to understand that to get give good advice, their Advisor needs time to think things over. Then the Advisor needs to patiently wait while the owner contemplates what they have been told.

Intuition

"At times you have to leave the city of your comfort and go into the wilderness of your intuition. What you'll discover will be wonderful. What you'll discover is yourself."

Alan Alda, [American Actor, director, screenwriter and author]

We experience intuition as an inner wisdom. We can sometime pick up inklings of its existence in our bodies, a "gut feeling." We have all experienced situations where we just "knew" what was right or what to do, but we could not explain it. And we have all had Eureka, "Aha!" moments when puzzles come together, confusion clears, ideas flow, and innovation sparks. Suddenly, you just "get it." It is like there was a small voice inside us.

**That voice of wisdom is there all the time;
we just need to learn how to listen.**

Intuition is the main way our unconscious mind communicates with us. Research has shown that our unconscious mind is far more powerful that our conscious mind. It is where our memories and experiences are stored. It is where we do most of our thinking.

> **INSIGHT:**
> *Rely on your instincts and decide on your intuition.*

Unfortunately, we are often taught to ignore our unconscious. In school, students get a lower grade if they cannot explain their answer. On the job, employees learn they must be able to justify their decisions. It often seems to be much safer to ignore intuition and just stick with what you can make other people understand.

The problem is that almost all great ideas and insights do not seem that great to most people. As we have said before, people in general like to stick with what they know. It is often difficult to absorb a new way of looking at something when you already have your own way of seeing it.

An Advisor must learn to use their intuition to find the powerful, creative solutions that the clients have been unable to find. If I cannot do this, I am of little use. As an Advisor, I have seen a variety of situations in a variety of diverse industries. Yet, even with that diversity of experience, I still can discern themes and patterns that I can draw upon later to solve other problems. When I do draw upon those patterns, I experience it as insight.

Facts and numbers can also create opportunities for intuition. In fact, I can often sense what may be going on in the company by studying the numbers on a financial statement. It seems to be like a sixth sense that defies logical examination. I've had CPA's and CFO's look at me with a raised eyebrow, unsure where my line of questioning is headed. But I generally get there with a bit of patience on their behalf. My path is roundabout but the fact remains: I just know. That knowingness leads to questions to test hypothesis and then "Viola!" There it is: an idea that makes sense.

Patience

"I like to tell people that all of our products and business will go through three phases. There's vision, patience, and execution."

Steve Ballmer, [CEO of Microsoft]

When it comes to transformation, patience is the most notewor-thy of the guiding virtues. Patience is the practice of making time your friend, not your enemy.

When circumstances in business cause an owner anxiety, discom-fort, suffering, or pain, the instinctual response is to act and do some-thing about it. Internally, fight or flight turns on. Second-guessing starts. We want to make the negative emotions go away and action often seems like the best way to do that. Or at least that's what we perceive.

The paradox of patience is that the very feeling that causes us discomfort is the same feeling that delivers insight.

The way I learned to create new options and innovative solutions was to put myself in the place of the owner and her circumstances using the virtue of compassion. In each case, I feel the pressures that the owner is under. I understand them because I have lived them. The power of patience though is to do the opposite. It is to stand still and confront the discomfort by acknowledging its presence and its validity in those circumstances. As I discussed earlier in this book, the virtue of patience is:

"Be comfortable with being uncomfortable."

What we *think* is the message of discomfort – to take the heat or pressure off – is not the answer. Our thinking leads us only to the same old patterns of behavior. From neuroscience we know the meddling of the conscious and reasoning cannot keep us on the surfboard, no more than it can provide us valuable insight. Ironically, solving complex business problems, creating

> **INSIGHT:**
> *To make great change, embrace what you most resist.*

new products, developing new ideas and bringing forth new concepts in business is the work of the emotional neural network. We cannot think our way out of discomfort. We must learn to use what neuroscience teaches us about our nature and apply it for our benefit. With patience, our unconscious responds with an answer to our questions. We just need to allow it.

The practice of patience in addition to compassion includes maintaining a keen awareness using a detached observation.

It is the understanding of how not to react to the craziness surrounding you. It is allowing inner discomfort to exist and to build momentum like a wave to create insight.

As the emotional wave builds, there comes a point at which it crests. And when the wave of emotion crests, you experience that wonderful moment of insight: Aha! Eureka! I've got it! Patience provides us the ability to use discomfort for positive purposes. Patience is the precursor of insight.

Some business owners may look at this virtue of patience and start to question how any business person in their right mind would apply it. I must agree it's not the John Wayne attitude I was brought up to believe about business ownership. The common perception of an owner responding to a gnawing financial concern is: Action! Action! We want action! Our business culture is based on doing something when things get difficult. What I am describing for a business owner is quite the opposite. It is our capacity as human beings to reflect and sit with the situation, if we want to pursue *the right answers*.

> **INSIGHT:**
> *If you don't take the time to do it right, you have to take the time to do it over!*

Emotions can be tricky when they run high in stressful situations. Patience teaches us to stay rooted and confront the frizzle-frazzle in our business lives, with the solid expectation that, if we just take the time, we can figure it out. Patience helps to deliver that nugget of gold. We just need to withstand the negative self-talk and fearful urges to immediately react.

❖   ❖   ❖

Chapter 10: On Becoming an Advisor - A Primer

❖ ❖ ❖

Introduction

This chapter is about the craft, the practice of being a Business Advisor and about what an owner should expect from an Advisor. In this chapter, I provide overviews of the role of the Advisor and the process I typically use for an advisory engagement. It is not the only process an Advisor might use, or even the best process under every circumstance. Rather, my intended point is that there is process involved which helps make the work efficient and understandable.

I do not intend this chapter to be an in-depth, all-encompassing, how-to training plan for Advisors. That can be found in other books. I just want to show an inside view about how an effective advisory relationship might work.

There is no guarantee that Advisor A using the same process, will get the same result as Advisor Z. That is because of their individual practices, experiences, and preferences. In fact, most Advisors utilize a variety of processes, depending upon the problem presented.

Becoming an Advisor

If one cannot become a skilled Advisor by getting an MBA (Master of Business Advice?), how does one become an Advisor? There are three components:

1. A firm grasp of the basics of business
2. A personal commitment to helping others
3. Experience, experience, and more experience with results

The first *can* be learned in business school. There is a great deal of value in business schools if the courses are taught by professors who have practical experience as well as academic credentials. An Advisor should also have a much broader basis of education than just business. History, English, Psychology, Physics, Mathematics, and Sociology all provide valuable perspectives, insights, and paradigms that can greatly enhance an Advisor's effectiveness in problem assessment, diagnosis, research, and analysis. The best Advisors are "Renaissance" people.

> **INSIGHT:**
> *The opportunity to explore who we are is created by what we do.*

The second component is personal. Someone either has that personal commitment to help others or they do not. Most people can feel whether or not another person really cares about them and their work. They can see it in the other person's eyes and how the person handles them self in a face-to-face meeting. Authenticity cannot be faked, at least not for very long. There's usually a seasoned maturity about a good Advisor. They exhibit confidence, security, thoughtfulness, and caring.

The third component, experience, must be earned, sometimes painfully. An effective Advisor has "been there." They may have operated at the "C" level or, preferably, have owned one or more businesses themselves. A credible Advisor also does not have a perfect track record. They need to have failed a couple of times. Someone who has never failed has likely never tested their limits or taken big risks.

Unless the Advisor has experienced failure *personally*, they cannot fully appreciate the feelings of a client in change or in crisis.

The Role of the Advisor

Advisors do not fix problems. Business decisions are the responsibility of the owner. The Advisor's role is to assist the owner to remedy problems and build the business by providing that owner with a bigger picture of:

- What is going on in and around the business.
- What alternatives are available to deal with the problem or take advantage of the opportunity.
- What the strengths, weaknesses, and potential impacts of each alternative are.

> **INSIGHT:**
> *The essence of business is trust: Everything else follows.*

As I explained in the previous chapter, the Advisor may take on several roles during an engagement: advisor, consultant, or coach, depending upon the circumstances. For example, the same individual can serve as Advisor to the owner, consultant to key management, and coach to front line staff.

The role of an Advisor requires a special internal discipline. The Advisor has no direct power or authority to make any changes or to control anything in an engagement. What the Advisor does have is influence. When interacting with the owner and their employees, establishing and maintaining that influence often requires being different with different people, providing what is needed to help each accomplish their task.

Even with the benefit of insight, an owner may not be able to see through the blockages of their past, self-interest, image, control, or emotional ties to embrace needed changes.

Old habits die hard, especially when those old habits were instrumental in early successes.

Successful change requires an inner commitment to accepting that business situations do not remain constant and what led to success yesterday can lead to disaster today. A critical part of the Advisor's role, therefore, is to remain committed to compassionately light the path for the owner, even when the owner is uncomfortable. It may take encouragement or a gentle nudge. It is precisely this growth that the owner may need.

The relationship between an owner and Advisor is always one of give and take. At times, the Advisor must defer to the owner's preferences. At other times, the Advisor may emphatically state and defend their opposing or differing view, using the information gleaned from their research. Sometimes the role of the Advisor is to validate the owner's judgment.

This interplay of forces – the give and take – often re-shapes into a new, combined perspective that becomes the foundation for real progress.

The value is clear: the owner gets a better result from the Advisor who is committed to what is in the best interests of the owner, not necessarily what's easy or what the owner may want to hear, see, or do. There's no room in the Advisor business for "yes men" or the faint of heart.

However, before overzealously entering choppy waters, I offer a word of caution. Whether or not an owner is willing to do something uncomfortable depends on the trust that has been built. The Advisor must ease the owner's fears or the needed changes will not be made. That trust must be built before there's even an attempt to embark on a risky, but needed, course of action or the owner's concentration will be on what they might lose, rather on what they might gain.

The larger the needed transformation, the more likely it will be that results may get worse before they get better. And successful change always takes time.

An experienced Advisor will build owner confidence by focusing on the little successes along the way.

Finally, there is a need for the Advisor to be aware of his/her own limitations. For instance, the Advisor's lesser industry knowledge may be a valid blind spot. The Advisor needs to be truthful when providing options to the owner with the caveat that he/she may not have a valid perspective due to the limitation of industry-specific knowledge. In fact, the owner may have more pertinent or relevant understanding when selecting an option that may not make complete sense to the Advisor. Communicating the truth about the above give-and-take usually establishes additional trust between the owner and Advisor.

The Advisory Engagement

The Beginning

Once an owner and an Advisor agree to work together, there is an initial phase where the two parties get to know each other. A skilled Advisor usually begins with a clear, written description of the process to be undertaken. This includes:

- The reason for the assignment and the goals to be achieved.
- Applicable time frames and deadlines.
  These should be based on the needs of the project, rather than arbitrarily set by the owner. Often the Advisor cannot tell how long a process will actually take until they are in the middle of it.
- The resources available.
- Access to personnel, including employees, managers, accountants, lawyers, and others as needed.
- Meetings between Advisor and owner – where and when.
- Mutual non-disclosures and, if applicable, non-compete agreements.
- What can and cannot be shared with specific others, especially employees.

While some of these may have been included in the Advisor's proposal or Letter of Engagement, it is usually a good idea to review the ground rules at the beginning. This discussion also helps alleviate the "FUD factor" (fear, uncertainty, and doubt) that often occurs when the engagement becomes a reality.

I have a set of questions for owners that I like to have answered before I begin work. These include:

1. How would you describe the circumstances you are currently facing?
2. What has your situation cost you so far?
3. What are you afraid will happen if nothing changes? What is your worst case scenario?
4. Where do you feel you want to be if you could resolve your situation? What is your best case scenario?
5. Are there any other areas where you see the potential for improvement?
6. What have you done so far about these issues?
7. Is there anything else you would like to tell me or that I should know?

Some of these will already have been discussed during the proposal process. What issues are still unclear will be discussed again until I have a clear understanding of where the owner is coming from. Great Advisors have to be great listeners. By the way, other Advisors are likely to have their own set of questions, which may be more specific based on their frame of reference.

In addition to the initial questions the Advisor is likely to ask, the following are examples of business areas where deeper questions may be asked, depending upon the type of business and the presenting problem:

- Company structure, ownership, entity type(s) and equity interests
- Other professionals (CPA, Legal, etc.)
- Financial statements
- Real property
- Metrics for the business
- Organizational charts

- Departmental processes
- Customers & markets
- Strategic & tactical plans
- Valuation & appraisals
- Vendors & suppliers

I also find it important right at the beginning to be clear that an Advisor relationship is a process, not an event. There will be ups and downs. There will be confusions and clarifications. There will be emotional reactions. In other words, it will be just like any other relationship. But if the parties remain honest and focused on achieving the best outcome for the owner and their business, there will also be trust, respect, and caring.

The Project

There are five main phases to any advisory engagement. These are:

1. **Discovery**

The purpose of the Discovery phase is to answer the question: "What is going on here?"

That is not a simple question for a number of reasons:

- The various people in the organization will have different perceptions about the nature, causes, and impacts of the problem or opportunity.
- There may be multiple causes and multiple impacts.
- Various people will be impacted by the issue in various ways.

- Various people may be impacted in different ways by different solutions and may be inclined to provide only that information that supports their best interest.
- Some people may withhold or spin information in order to avoid blame or enhance their position.

In other words, each of the people within, and outside, an organization will have their *personal* interests and may, consciously or unconsciously, skew the information the Advisor receives. A big part of the art of business advising is being able to sort through these biases to arrive at the underlying truth.

Another important part of Discovery is what I call Root Cause Analysis. It is often quite easy to look at an issue and see the immediate precedent cause. For example, if revenues have remained constant and profits are down, the obvious thing to do is cut costs. The temptation is to stop there and focus all change efforts on that. A skilled Advisor, however, will keep on digging until they get to the deepest level or Root Cause of the problem. A more careful analysis might show that revenues are constant because the sales force is overextended. Competitors' sales are rising. Investing in new salespeople, sales training, and/or sales automation to boost the revenue side may be a much better strategy than cost cutting.

2. Alternatives

Once the problem has been agreed upon and the Root Cause identified, the next step is to come up with alternative ways of dealing with the issue. In other words, what are the possible approaches to solving this problem or taking advantage of this opportunity?

Sometimes, the answer is clear and the problem becomes solely one of implementation (although that often presents its own problems). More often, however, there are various ways that the problem or opportunity can be approached. These alternatives are of three types:

1. The way things are being done in the company now. This may, in fact, be the root cause of the problem in the first place.
2. The ways things are done in the industry. Taking one of these alternatives may help the problem, but common industry practices rarely create competitive advantages.
3. The "out-of-the-box" solutions that a skilled Advisor can help find.

In addition to addressing the problem, a skilled Advisor will take a step further and ask "Is there an opportunity buried inside this problem?" If one company has a particular type of problem, it is likely that competitors in the same industry face similar problems. If an Advisor can help find a new, unique solution to that type of problem, one that competitors are unlikely to utilize, the company now has a competitive advantage.

3. Assessment

Before an owner can make an informed decision as to which alternative to take, they need to understand the pros and cons of each. These must be understood not only as they apply to the issue being addressed, but also in terms of the implications a decision might have on other parts of the organization or the organization as a whole.

A skilled Advisor will base their assessment of alternatives on:

- The best information they can get
- The owners vision and preferences
- The Advisor's own insights and experiences

4. Recommendations

There are many ways to present recommendations to an owner. Some Advisors prefer to make a formal presentation at the end of the assessment phase. Others, like me, prefer to keep the owner updated on an ongoing basis. That way, there are few surprises when the final recommendations are made. Also, owners often have valuable insights and experiences that only come out when out-of-the-box ideas are presented.

The most important part of the recommendations phase is truth. My recommendations to owners often include things that owners may not want to hear. If the Advisory engagement is to be successful, the owner needs to trust what the Advisor says.

At the same time, a skilled Advisor is never insensitive to the feelings of the owner. Respect and tact are critical. For example, rather than saying "Here's what you should do," I typically would say "Have you considered...?" or "Would ...... be a possibility?"

As I have stated many times before, the final decision is the owner's, NOT the Advisor's, and there can be big differences between what the owner believes and what the Advisor sees.

The Advisor is responsible for doing the best research and analysis they can and for presenting their findings clearly. Then the Advisor needs to let go.

While the owner's personal preferences, biases, fears, etc. are relevant to the decision, the Advisor must be careful not to become emotionally invested in being "right." As soon as that happens, objectivity and compassion can be lost and those attitudes are essential to the Advisor's effectiveness.

If the owner decides to take a course of action different from the one recommended by the Advisor, that is the owner's choice. However, if the owner elects a different path because the Advisor has not done a good job of research, analysis, or presentation, then that is the Advisor's failure.

4. **Follow On**

Once the owner has made the final decision about how they want to approach a certain issue, the Advisor can then choose to:

- **Leave and go on to the next assignment**

  This might be the best choice if the Advisor believes the owner has made a poor decision and does not feel it would be ethical to remain and assist in further damaging the company. The Advisor might also leave if they do not have the skills the owner requires for implementation, the owner has no further problems they want to address, or the owner chooses not to continue the engagement for whatever reason

- **Assist the owner with implementing the decision**

  Once a path of action has been decided upon, the Advisor can take on the roles of consultant and/or coach to assist in implementation. Advisors can be in a very good place to do this. The Advisor will have built trust with the

owner and, usually, other key people in the organization. The Advisor understands the benefits and risks of
the choice and does not have to be brought up to speed.
Finally, the Advisor usually has an emotional interest in
seeing the problem finally resolved or the opportunity
exploited.

- **Address the owners next problem or opportunity**
  The Advisor may also remain in the strictly Advisory role and
  continue to work on other issues or opportunities that the
  owner is interested in or that have been uncovered in the
  first engagement.

A vital component of resolving the initial issue is maintaining a
sense of urgency going forward. Once pain of any kind goes away,
it is human nature to want to quit and relax for a while. The initial
effort will undoubtedly have identified other issues and opportunities that can be efficiently addressed while the momentum is
already there.

Expectations & Metrics

Establishing expectations and measuring results is the core "business" part of an advisory relationship. Expectations, metrics, and
commitment should be set early and revisited often as progress is
made and/or the situation changes.

Clear accountability can be difficult in advisory relationships.
While the gathering of information, the assessment of options, and
the making of recommendations are the responsibility of the Advisor,

it is the owner that makes the final decision and makes resources available for its implementation. And owners do not always do what Advisors recommend nor are they always willing to invest the resources required.

Therefore, accountability must be the responsibility of the owner/Advisor relationship and each party needs to accept that while neither one can make things work on their own, either one can ruin things.

I follow the following outline when setting metrics for my Advisory work:

1. Metrics are clear and objectively measurable.
2. Metrics are focused on the problem or opportunity at hand, rather than on individual contributions.
3. Avoid credit stealing & blame game.
4. Metrics reflect both the pain AND the vision of the owner.
5. Metrics include opportunity costs/risks of NOT acting. What is this problem costing you? This month? This year? Long term?
6. Metrics can evolve as Advisor and owner build mutual trust.
7. Metrics measure ROI wherever possible. Business advice is an investment, not an expense.

The End of a Project

Advisory engagements have a beginning and they also have an end. At the end of an engagement, or even a project within an engagement, holding a wrap up session with all involved is important. It puts closure to any loose ends of the project and provides clarity for the owner's path forward. This is sometimes known as the "hand-off." In some cases, there's a written report describing what was accomplished by the Advisor and the project team. In other cases, closure will be an event, such as a succession in leadership, a sale, or an acquisition.

For some engagements, results may be quantifiable: for example, lower costs, higher profits, or consequence avoidance. In other cases, outcomes may be realized through people, process, technology, or strategy. If the engagement began as the result of a crisis, the outcome may be the fact the business withstood a serious internal or external event and can return to normal, or even improved, operations.

There is variability in every advisory engagement. Even the best laid plans provide for some wiggle room under fire, because executions are seldom flawless and external situations usually change as progress is made. In the end, what is important is that each involved party feels they have accomplished something of value for their investment of time, money, and personal effort.

❖ ❖ ❖

Chapter 11: Reflections on Insight & Advice

❖ ❖ ❖

At this point in our journey, it is my hope is that you have gained some insight of your own from the advisory experiences I have shared, and that in some small way, my observations and personal journey have helped illuminate your own business path. What follows in this chapter is a final collection of my thoughts and outlooks on the importance of insight and advice in business.

Leading Business Change

Alchemy is an influential philosophical tradition whose practitioners have, from antiquity, claimed it to be the precursor to profound powers. The defining objectives of alchemy are varied; these include the creation of the fabled "philosopher's stone", the ability to transform base metals into the noble metals: gold or silver. The philosophers' stone was the central symbol of the mystical terminology of alchemy, symbolizing perfection at its finest, enlightenment, and heavenly bliss. Efforts to discover the philosophers' stone were known as *The Magnum Opus* (The "Great Work") from Wikipedia.

Using alchemy as a metaphor, business change occurs by applying the "philosopher's stone" at different business transition points.

These transition points may present as: a financial crisis, being stuck, a loss of leadership, apathy, inertia, or any number of other business states where business progress is faltering. (Remember, business progress is different than profits.)

Many times this desire for change comes from either vision or fear. In practical terms, alchemy in business is the process of turning fear to possibilities, dreams into reality, being stuck into insights, inaction into results, and underachievement into high performance. It is a business art that uses financial outcomes as a measure for accountability.

The insights in business mean using both what we see (financial measures) and what we don't see (possibilities, motivations, strengths and desires).

I believe strongly in the "human wildcard" of ordinary people that become the catalyst for changing the perceived reality. Why? Because that wildcard has an openness and propensity for something that is deeply valuable: insight and innovation.

And let me clarify, I don't sit around the office, my head in the clouds with incense burning, wearing a long robe, pondering problems in isolation, listening to mood music. (That's reserved for alone time.) But that's also not the way to gain insight. I am actively engaged with people, questioning, observing, and formulating possibilities as I go. I respect each person as a chalice of potential for change. I proceed without a pre-conceived notion or canned solution. I've proven it works, particularly where others before me have failed. It is my openness and

freshness, without the limitations of the blind spots carried by preconceptions of a certain industry. The rules I apply are universal. I deal
with unpredictability and circumstances, and set a stage for energizing
the existence of possibilities, options, and solutions.

Business Transformation

Transformation occurs in people and systems due to higher levels of awareness and understanding of one's circumstances, coupled
with keen observation for finding ways through or around a crisis or
problem. Change comes from contemplation, with the unconscious
working behind the scenes to present options and solutions at a later
time as intuition and insight.

I may not change your concept of the value of business advice if you
say, *"No, there's no room for gaining insight in my business."* If there's a
possibility to influence you, it may only be my timing, so read on.

In an age of speed and technology, I believe business has
higher risks associated with it, especially after the economic col-
lapse since 2008. Foremost in my mind, we've lost the fine art of
being intimately connected to one another. It's now a technology
experience.

**We've been told by technologists, the media, and Wall Street
that being connected with our people takes too much time
(face-to-face), is taboo (liabilities), and creates
complexities (relationships).**

And yet it's precisely what we need integrated into our business
life. Why?

Consider that great innovations, discoveries, and endeavors start with a person.

Because a person may have refused to accept the *status quo*, they went on to find a new way of thinking, doing, or being. As owners, we invest "all-in" and expect the same from those to whom we are stewards. So why not develop that potentiality?

Seeing the value of insight is much more obvious when a business goes haywire. We are confronted with a complex adversity and we try to immediately fix it. Much to our dismay, this immediate fixing doesn't work. We find the matter has a mind of its own, and known solutions seem to elude us time and time again. I like to use a metaphor for business difficulty as hand-rolling a bale of hay wire. As we roll tighter and tighter to create order in the roll, the tension builds and builds, until the wire slips out of our hands, time after time. The force of tension springs the order that we had intended, and ends up as an unmanageable tangled mess. All we did was waste our time, become frustrated, and lose more wire (assets).

I believe that business owners have been "rolling wire" for several years now by working on the visible – cutting excess costs, reducing labor, eliminating levels of support, leaning out – all which have led us to the spring point of holding onto the haywire...barely. So I ask, why continue to try and hold onto the haywire?

It may be that we need to assess the value of disorder, and the tangled mess, to see how it might serve us.

Quite possibly, the solutions we then adopt may come with less tension, allowing us to develop even more new insights. And then we can attack what's next.

Clients get immersed in the "reality" of their situation. They don't get an ironclad guarantee that they get everything they want.

Sometimes they get more, much more than they anticipated. And at other times, they get most of what they wanted or expected, but not everything.

Generally, that's the best that can be obtained, given each business' unique circumstances. But in every case, the situation transforms dramatically from one state to another. And that leaves options for business renewal and rejuvenation.

Building on Trust

An article from the Harvard Business Review has been saved in one of my folders for over 10 years. In it, excerpts are taken from the book, _Management Challenges for the 21st Century_, by Peter F. Drucker. The article is titled <u>Managing Oneself</u>. In that article, Drucker points out that over a 50-year working life, one must be able to learn how to manage, develop, and position themselves to make the greatest work life contribution.

He goes on to support this premise by advocating strengths assessment, working in ways that people best perform, and not trying to force individual change to gain a result. In other words, Drucker suggests, as I have experienced and many of my clients have applied, that the best results are from applying strengths to the requirements of the position to gain high performance.

Drucker goes on to say that in order to manage oneself the key question to ask is: What are my values? I presented the Virtue of

Integrity as I believe it is the foundation of building trust in business. Drucker's insight resonates for me in the following:

> *"Organizations are no longer built on force, but on trust. The existence of trust between people does not necessarily mean that they like one another. It means that they understand one another. Taking responsibility for relationships is therefore an absolute necessity. It is a duty. One owes that responsibility to all one's co-workers: those whose work one depends on as well as those who depend on one's own work."*

Drucker then concludes that, *"In a society in which success has become so terribly important, having options will become increasingly vital."* This is precisely what I have found as a value in the advisory work I perform:

**Options and solutions that previously were unforeseen
and then brought to light, have the power to
transform the present.**

Pulling Together

My entire business journey has been one of identifying the resources I have as intellectual, physical, and spiritual (mind, hands and heart) and putting that entire base of resources in service. The personal in business as I may describe it (heart/emotion/spirit/ unconscious) has untapped potential to provide answers and guidance for us. The bottom line is that business as a human activity is most effective when one puts their entire humanity into the work. My clients and I have witnessed remarkable changes that occur in businesses that should have and would have otherwise failed. And applying my Guiding Virtues has resulted in remarkable change for the better.

Many owners feel stuck or in crisis because they want to do everything themselves. They may be embarrassed or afraid of asking for help because they are hardest on themselves. What they've learned is to *push* themselves harder and harder.

**Why do we push so hard when that effort sacrifices
the very quality of life we are striving to earn?**

It reminds me of an instructor of soccer coaches who observed a seasoned coach making his team run laps. He questioned why? The seasoned coach said that it built endurance. The instructor remarked that running laps doesn't teach anyone to be a better soccer player, only a better lapper. That made me consider what we were practicing in business.

Like the lap runners, we may become better pushers by pushing, but business doesn't necessarily respond very well to expert pushing. When it comes to people in business they generally resist and protect themselves from being pushed.

What do we teach new entrepreneur owners in business schools? The answers are: critical thinking, process, data mining, and analysis. It is true that those skills are a part of the answer to performance improvements and change relies on those metrics and visible measures.

However, I believe it is of equal value is to know the practices of pulling - internally or externally - the unseen potentialities from a situation, those resources which may not be apparent from purely analytics.

That's the magic and art of transition and transformation. It's getting those numbers or themes to talk to us and give us the message.

This area of insight development for graduate students and business owners is completely missing. There is great value in having deeper understanding how to develop rich solutions in business, than in figuring out how to beat the system, numbers or process. Rote answers and short memories tend to repeat failures. Just take a look at Wall Street. We have all suffered the consequences of losing virtue in business. In today's age of complexity, we can no longer afford the easy answers. There is much more to know and understand than any one of us can handle. Therefore, we must all pull together.

The Challenges Forward

If I've been able to make any point by this work, I hope that it resonates with you that there is more to owning and operating a business than what conventional knowledge teaches. Unseen potentiality exists in each and every business and we need to be able to access that potential.

I'm convinced with all our business shortcomings and strengths, and the complexities involved with owning and operating a business, our reliance on insight today is more critical than ever before.

The art of business success must concentrate on contributions made by the totality of the potential resources we have available in our organizations, starting with each person's heart, hands, and mind. The virtues we live and the personality of our business must shine through to others in the fogginess of daily information overload. And we must stay connected with meaning, purpose, and mission, rooted in our values in a world that at times ignores these higher values. May you take this road of self-reliance knowing that there are others who can make a difference in your journey.

Everyday situations in starting a business, staying in business, or exiting a business demand more of us. We expect that boomer owners will be starting new part-time businesses or keeping their existing businesses longer due to today's difficulties in achieving a comfortable retirement. Going it alone in business without some form of business advice can be costly and is unrealistic with the complexities of business we face every day. There's no need to suffer in isolation when so many options abound. It's just a matter of finding the right path that makes the most sense in pursuing. It's there. Our mission is to find it.

I see the value of integrating insights in business as a significant, competitive factor. In the process of applying the virtues of advice, there's an opportunity for making breakthroughs in creative problem-solving and innovation. By educating others, I see the value in how to better identify and work through the unseen problems of business that are blockages of progress. I see the value of deep practice that takes off tension, especially for the owner.

I expect our individual work horizons to be longer than any generation before us. I also expect to be in better health, in a large part to scientific advances and healthcare technology. There is a $10 Trillion challenge of business succession over the next 15 years as boomer owner's turnover their businesses to the next generation. For the 7 million privately-held businesses and their stakeholders, I also envision a higher quality of business life, which better handles downside risks and uncaps upside potentials.

I believe that insight is where entrepreneurs and owners, great individual achievers and great organizations find their touchstone.

It's in an ability to tap this core aspect of our humanness. We must shepherd that process along with a growth and abundance mindset. We all have the potential for solutions to problems – it's getting people engaged and invested in the practice of developing insight, so solutions begin to appear. It's also living forward in business as a learning leader, rather than a rearview follower. It's our outlook on this great experiment of business that matters. If we succumb to the fear of what we don't know or understand it only means one path: out of fear comes defense. Out of defense comes reluctance to change. Out of that reluctance come isolation and obsolescence. It's a downward spiral.

As business leaders and owners, we decide to incorporate insight into our practice of being in business.

We can patiently sit with our misery and be comfortable being uncomfortable, allowing the practices of our virtues to inspire us, while our personal and business potentials unfold. We are not required to cater to the fear-mongering of others. Lightning strikes when insight comes together with tangible results.

Once a business transformation is experienced, there's an eternal knowingness that you can navigate through almost any difficulty. It's a very, very valuable personal asset. We must first decide to love learning. Because out of the love of learning comes collaboration. Out of collaboration comes community. Out of community comes integration. And a business that has its strengths integrated and applied is unstoppable.

Coda

Thank you for joining me on this journey.

If you found any beneficial INSIGHT in this book, please LET ME KNOW! I would really appreciate a short review from you. (Critiques are also welcome.) www.davidwimer.com.

Your help in spreading the word about INSIGHT is gratefully received. You'll also find advice, promotions, webinars, seminars and release specials at: www.davidwimer.com.

Finally, here is my wish for you:

> *"May you have insight on your journey of business;*
> *May wisdom illuminate your way when*
> *navigating any business transition; and*
> *May you confront complexity with the peace of*
> *mind that any challenge may be overcome by*
> *applying the guiding virtues of advice."*

Insightfully Yours,
David Wimer

❖   ❖   ❖

www.ingramcontent.com/pod-product-compliance
Lightning Source LLC
Chambersburg PA
CBHW060547200326
41521CB00007B/512